Understanding the
US-Iran Crisis

Understanding the US-Iran Crisis

A Primer

Phyllis Bennis

OLIVE
BRANCH
PRESS

An imprint of Interlink Publishing Group, Inc.
www.interlinkbooks.com

First published in 2009 by

OLIVE BRANCH PRESS
An imprint of Interlink Publishing Group, Inc.
46 Crosby Street, Northampton, Massachusetts 01060
www.interlinkbooks.com

Library of Congress Cataloging-in-Publication Data
Bennis, Phyllis.
Understanding the US–Iran crisis : a primer / by Phyllis Bennis. —
1st American ed.
p. cm.
Includes bibliographical references.
ISBN 978-1-56656-731-2 (pbk.)
1. Middle East—Relations—United States. 2. United States—Relations—
Middle East. 3. United States—Relations—Iran. 4. Iran—Relations—United
States. 5. Nuclear arms control—Iran. 6. United States—Military policy. 7.
United States—Politics and government—2001– 8. Iran—Politics and
government—1997– I. Title.
DS63.2.U5B4455 2008
327.73055—dc22
2008030370

Book design by Juliana Spear

Cover image: Iranian men chant Islamic slogans, as they mourn, in Tehran,
February 28, 2008, during a funeral ceremony of five members of armed
forces, who were killed during 1980–88 Iran–Iraq war, whose remains
have recently been recovered. (AP Photo/Vahid Salemi)

Printed and bound in the United States of America
10 9 8 7 6 5 4 3 2 1

To request our complete 40-page full-color catalog,
please call us toll free at 1-800-238-LINK, visit our website at
www.interlinkbooks.com or write to Interlink Publishing
46 Crosby Street, Northampton, MA 01060

Contents

PART III—ALTERNATIVES TO WAR

Preface

This book goes to press as the last weeks of George W. Bush's administration tick away. The Bush years have been characterized by some of the most reckless and dangerous acts of militarism and unilateralism in US history, all in pursuit of a new version of US empire to assert global control over strategic resources, especially oil, and to expand US power, especially through military bases. The disastrous illegal invasion and occupation of Iraq took pride of place by far in Bush's crusade.

And while the Bush administration is finally on its way out, the Iraq war will certainly continue under a new administration. None of the candidates for the 2008 presidential election intend to end the Iraq war. Republican John McCain, who said he envisioned US troops in Iraq for perhaps 100 years, has campaigned as the major congressional defender of and cheerleader for Bush's war. And while both Democratic candidate Barack Obama and Hillary Clinton, his one-time rival for the nomination, claim they would "end the war," their virtually identical plans would leave between 35,000 and 80,000 US troops in Iraq for an indeterminate length of time.

The White House has not learned the lessons of the Iraq war's failure, of the death and destruction it has brought to the Iraqi people, as well as the hundreds of thousands of US soldiers badly injured (physically or mentally) or the thousands killed in the war. Failure in Iraq did not diminish the Bush administration's reliance on war as its first choice in responding to international challenges. The crisis the Bush administration has created with its belligerence toward Iran continues to intensify, and the threat of a new US war in the Middle East continues to dangerously destabilize the region. The 2008 elections will not bring an end to that crisis, although the end of the Bush extremism and the coming of a new administration may—if we fight for it—provide new opportunities for greater public engagement in the process and increase the possibility of resolving the crisis without war.

But that is only a possibility. So at this moment of potential political change, it remains of vital importance to examine the shape of the current US–Iran crisis, to understand something of its historical underpinning, to demand that critical public voices be heard. It can be difficult to find the information needed to answer the cries for war. But the danger remains too great to do any less.

With George W. Bush's administration in its last weeks in office, the danger of a US military attack on Iran still looms as a dangerous possibility. Widespread official government, military, and analytical sources, including the collective assessment of all sixteen US intelligence agencies, have debunked the various pretexts being asserted to justify such an attack. But the continuing, ideologically driven extremism in the White House means that the danger of a reckless, unilateral military attack remains, and such an attack could happen despite the consequences.

Most Americans—and virtually everyone else around the world—are opposed to such a strike. Widening opposition to the illegal US war in Iraq, growing recognition that the war in Afghanistan has failed to bring stability or democracy to that beleaguered country, new tensions rising in Pakistan, escalating violence and humanitarian crisis in the Israeli-occupied Palestinian territories, have all brought new fears. But the crisis has also created heightened interest in the wider Middle Eastern region, in nuclear dangers, and especially in Iran. This book, written with the assistance of the Iran Team at the Institute for Policy Studies in Washington—John Cavanagh, Farrah Hassen, Erik Leaver, Saif Rahman, and Marc Raskin—is designed to address some of those fears, answer some of those questions, and propose some ideas to prevent those looming disasters.

Introduction

Washington watched as 2007 came to a violent and inglorious end. US wars raged in Iraq and Afghanistan; the US-backed Israeli occupation suffocated Palestinians; US-allied governments in Pakistan and Kenya faced national explosions over false democratization and stolen elections; the policies of US corporations fueled poverty and resource wars across Africa. Powerful forces in the US had already begun to critically reassess what they saw as the diminishing value of the Bush administration's reckless global interventionism.

By the end of the year, that elite divide—with the Bush White House increasingly isolated and discredited—had shown up in a leaked story of how Bush's CIA hid and then destroyed videotapes documenting the interrogation-by-torture of detainees in the so-called global war on terror. There was an explosive story documenting how Bush's billions of dollars in "anti-terrorism" military aid to Pakistan had completely failed to help stabilize that war-wracked country. Another leak exposed widespread damning views that the US and its allies were losing the war in Afghanistan, the invasion and occupation that were supposed to shine as Washington's "good war"—the war that no one could criticize because of September 11.

But the most important evidence of the split within the powerful elites came on December 3, 2007, with the release of a new National Intelligence Estimate on Iran. The NIE, reflecting the consensus view of all 16 US intelligence agencies, made clear that Iran did not have a nuclear weapon, did not have a program to build a nuclear weapon, and was less determined to develop nuclear weapons than US intelligence agencies had earlier claimed.

When the NIE was released there was a sigh of relief from many quarters—in the US and around the world. How could anyone now claim there was any legal or moral pretext for threatening Iran? But somehow the NIE did not stop Washington's talk of war. Two days after the NIE was released, the *Washington Post* headline read "U.S. Renews Efforts to Keep Coalition Against Tehran."[1] The White House, the president, and especially the vice president continued ratcheting up the rhetoric. In fact, the president had been told of the NIE's overall conclusions months earlier, back in the summer of 2007.

When Bush arrived in the Middle East in January 2008 for his first trip to Israel as president, Iran remained on the top of the agenda. One of his primary goals was to reassure Israel that the NIE had not changed US policy toward Iran, and that despite the intelligence agencies' consensus that Iran was not building a nuclear weapon, "all options" remained on the table. According to *Newsweek*, "in private conversations with Israeli Prime Minister Ehud

Olmert last week, the president all but disowned the document, said a senior administration official who accompanied Bush on his six-nation trip to the Mideast. 'He told the Israelis that he can't control what the intelligence community says, but that [the NIE's] conclusions don't reflect his own views.'" *Newsweek* went on to recognize that

> Bush's behind-the-scenes assurances may help to quiet a rising chorus of voices inside Israel's defense community that are calling for unilateral military action against Iran. Olmert, asked by *Newsweek* after Bush's departure on Friday whether he felt reassured, replied: "I am very happy." ... Bush told Olmert he was uncomfortable with the findings and seemed almost apologetic. Bush's national-security adviser, Stephen Hadley, told reporters in Jerusalem that Bush had only said to Olmert privately what he's already said publicly, which is that he believes Iran remains "a threat" no matter what the NIE says. But the president may be trying to tell his allies something more: that he thinks the document [the NIE] is a dead letter. [2]

Just a couple of days before President George W. Bush's first trip to Israel—in January 2008, in the last year of his presidency—the Pentagon reported an "incident" in the Strait of Hormuz. Iranian speed boats had allegedly swarmed between three large US warships heading into the Persian Gulf, broadcasting threatening messages that the US ships were about to explode and dropping small box-like objects into the seas. Just as the sailors were aiming their guns at the provocateurs, we were told, the Iranian boats reversed course and sped away.

Reuters described how the boats "aggressively approached" the US ships. The Pentagon called the boats' actions "careless, reckless and potentially hostile,"[3] the White House "reckless and provocative."[4] Numerous Persian speakers pointed out that the voice making the threats did not sound as though it had a Persian accent. The US Navy itself acknowledged that they had no idea where the voice making the threats had actually come from. Quickly the words "Tonkin Gulf incident" were on many lips. Many remembered August 4, 1964, the "attack on a US Naval ship" that Lyndon Johnson used as a pretext for sending troops to Vietnam. Years later the world learned that the alleged attack had never occurred at all; it was cooked up. Would the "swarming boat incident" in the Strait of Hormuz serve as George Bush's Tonkin Gulf?

Not immediately. But the rhetorical escalations continued. In March 2008 Admiral William Fallon, chief of Central Command, resigned from the military following his highly public disagreement with Bush administration threats of a military attack on Iran. A day later, Vice President Dick Cheney went to the Middle East, ostensibly to encourage Israeli and Palestinian negotiators, but clearly aiming at pressing allies in the region to accept Washington's escalations against Iran. The likelihood of a military strike increased again.

In early April General David Petraeus and Ambassador Ryan Crocker, top commander and US envoy in Iraq respectively, reported to Congress that their "surge" strategy of sending 30,000 additional US troops to occupy Iraq was succeeding. But the enemy in Iraq was changing, they said: no longer is al-Qaeda the main problem; now Iran has emerged in that role. Bush administration officials began talking of a "proxy war" in Iraq, in which Iran is arming and training various Shi'a militia, including "special groups" within Moqtada al-Sadr's Mahdi Army, as a way of attacking the US.

The media drumbeat soon followed. On April 12, just a few days after the congressional hearings, the *New York Times* headline, referring to an interview with Crocker, read "Iran Is Fighting Proxy Battle in Iraq, U.S. Diplomat Says."[5] The lead front-page article in the *Washington Post* the same day was titled "Iran Top Threat to Iraq, U.S. Says." It began: "Last week's violence in Basra and Baghdad has convinced the Bush administration that actions by Iran, and not al-Qaeda, are the primary threat inside Iraq, and has sparked a broad reassessment of policy in the region, according to senior U.S. officials."[6] The next day the lead editorial warned that "the proxy war in Iran is just one front in a much larger Iranian offensive," and went on to link activities of Hamas in Gaza, Hezbollah within the Lebanese parliament, and Iraq's own nuclear power enrichment activities as equally the responsibility of Iran's "offensive."[7] The same day the

New York Times ran an op-ed by a leading Israeli strategist calling for the US to recognize Israel's right to attack Iran independently.[8]

President Bush accepted Petraeus and Crocker's recommendations and embraced their claims regarding Iran's "malign" role, saying, "Iraq is the convergence point for two of the greatest threats to America in this new century: Al-Qaeda and Iran." He then sent Petraeus and Crocker back to Iraq—but ordered them to stop off in Saudi Arabia. He sent other diplomats on simultaneous visits to other Arab capitals, supposedly to encourage greater engagement with Iraq, but clearly primarily to urge support for the rising US threats against Iran.

And to broaden further the US crusade against Iran, on April 17, 2008, Republican and Bush-supporting Florida Congressman Mario Diaz-Balart introduced a new amendment to the just-passed "jubilee" bill that would provide debt relief to two dozen impoverished countries. The amendment, supported by 291 members of Congress, stated that countries—any countries, including the two dozen desperately poor ones most in need of debt relief—"that have a business relationship with Iran are not eligible to be considered under this debt relief program." That would likely eliminate most of the countries eligible, since Iran is a major global oil supplier, and "south–south" commercial ties have been a longstanding feature of Iranian trade. Potential beneficiaries of debt relief would be forced to choose between accepting US assistance and continuing trade with Iran. How much real "free choice" do we think would be reflected in that decision?

It was going to be a long campaign. Despite the NIE confirming Iran did not have and was not building a nuclear weapon, despite the reports of "backdoor" discussions between US and Iranian representatives, it remained clear that neither intelligence estimates nor actual facts on the ground in Iran or the region would determine Bush administration policy towards Iran. The possibility of a US military strike on Iran remains a very real threat.

—PART I—

THE CURRENT CRISIS

Is Iran a threat to the United States?

The Bush administration has claimed, almost since coming into office, that Iran is a "threat" to the US. Even US intelligence agencies agree that Iran doesn't possess nuclear weapons or a nuclear weapons program, and that it is very unclear whether Iran even wants to build such a weapon. Iran has never threatened the United States. (And unlike many countries in its neighborhood, Iran has not invaded another country in over a century.)

In 2007, according to the CIA, Iran spent about $5.1 billion on its military—about 2.5 percent of its GDP. The US, on the other hand, spent $626 billion on the military that same year, amounting to 4.5 percent of its GDP of $13.7 *trillion*. More relevant, perhaps, the US spent almost half of the total of global arms spending—about 46 percent. So Iran does not represent a strategic military threat to the United States or to Americans.

In 2005 Mahmoud Ahmadinejad, the populist former mayor of Tehran, was elected president of Iran. His rhetoric, aimed primarily at his younger and poorer supporters, remained fiery, often even offensive, including questioning whether the Nazi Holocaust had really happened. But his overall populist, anti-Western approach brought him significant public support at home, where unemployment was high and opportunities few.

Not surprisingly, US and other Western media and political figures exaggerated his actual rhetoric.

Ahmadinejad's political opposition to Israel has never been in doubt, but still his statements were distorted. Outrage erupted across the US and Europe in October 2005 following the claim that Ahmadinejad had threatened to "wipe Israel off the map." Israel's then Prime Minister Ariel Sharon called for Iran to be expelled from the United Nations; a few months later Israeli Vice Prime Minister and Nobel Peace Laureate Shimon Peres said, "the president of Iran should remember that Iran can also be wiped off the map."[9]

But as it turned out, Ahmadinejad had not said those words at all. "Ahmadinejad did not say he was going to wipe Israel off the map because no such idiom exists in Persian," Juan Cole, a Middle East expert at the University of Michigan told the *New York Times*. "He did say he hoped its regime, i.e., a Jewish-Zionist state occupying Jerusalem, would collapse." Cole went on to note that since Iran has not "attacked another country aggressively for over a century, I smell the whiff of war propaganda."[10]

Just as the NIE, which would debunk Bush's favorite claims about Iran as a nuclear threat, was being finalized, new assertions began to emerge from the White House that Iran was directly responsible for killing Americans in Iraq, ostensibly through providing Iraqi resistance forces with some of the powerful explosives used in the roadside bombs that were killing significant numbers of US troops. No evidence of Iranian involvement was ever made public; from their origin in early 2006 the claims were limited to unsubstantiated assertions by military and government officials. But the notion of Iran as a direct threat to the US began to spread.

The Bush administration began to use the language of the earlier 2005 NIE as the basis for its escalation against Iran, despite the fact that the report provided at best tenuous support for Washington's aggression. The NIE's conclusion focused on the dangers of Iran "*acquiring and mastering technologies* that could be diverted to bombmaking." The bar had been dramatically lowered. No longer would the Bush administration threaten military strikes only to prevent Iran from building a nuclear weapon. Now, according to the president, the strikes would be legitimate and even necessary to prevent Iran from even acquiring knowledge of nuclear technology. In April 2006 Bush ominously warned that "the world is united and concerned about their [Iran's] desire to have not only a nuclear weapon, but the capacity to make a nuclear weapon or *the knowledge as to how to make a nuclear weapon*, all of which we're working hard to convince them not to try to achieve." And in the same press conference he repeated, just in case anyone missed it the first time: "we've agreed on the goal, and that is the Iranians should not have a nuclear weapon, the capacity to make a nuclear weapon, *or the knowledge* as to how to make a nuclear weapon."[11]

The significance of that language lay in the uncontested reality that Iran already *had*, indeed has had for many years, "the knowledge as to how to make a nuclear weapon." Not only because much of that knowledge is available on the internet, but because the basic technology needed to enrich uranium for nuclear power is the same as that required for nuclear weapons. Of course it is easier to carry out the 3–5 percent enrichment needed for nuclear power than the 90-plus percent enrichment necessary to produce weapons-grade uranium. But the technology is the same. Once you have the knowledge to build and run the centrifuges to enrich uranium, you just need time and money and practice to enrich enough for a bomb. You also do need missile technology, but like many countries around the world, Iran already had that, too. Bush's bar for bombing Iran could hardly get any lower.

Does Iran have nuclear weapons or a nuclear weapons program?

No. Iran does not and has never had a nuclear weapon— and no one, not even the Bush administration, claims it has. Despite claims by the Bush administration and others, there is also no evidence Iran has a military program to build nuclear weapons. And even the Bush administration's own intelligence agencies acknowledged in the December 2007 National Intelligence Estimate that the weapons program they claim once existed had been ended by 2003.

Iran does have an active nuclear power program, including a program to enrich uranium to fuel the program. Iran was one of the original signatories to the 1968 Nuclear Non-Proliferation Treaty (NPT), and like all other "non–nuclear weapons states" that signed the treaty, Iran has a legal right to produce and use nuclear power for peaceful purposes.[12] But although Iran has a legal right to nuclear power, the US still doesn't like it, and Washington has pressured other countries to impose UN Security Council sanctions against Iran for exercising that internationally guaranteed right.

The stance of the IAEA, the UN's nuclear watchdog agency, has remained consistent: despite what it identified as some ambiguities and the need for greater transparency regarding Iran's past nuclear programs, the IAEA has repeatedly stated from the beginning that its inspectors on the ground have never found evidence that Iran is diverting nuclear facilities to military use.[13]

There is a sharp irony in history, in that the US once actively supported Iran's nuclear ambitions. From the mid-1970s the US government was engaged in urging Iran, then ruled by the US-backed shah, to build nuclear power plants with the specific goal of expanding Iran's energy base beyond oil. In his history of Iran's nuclear program, professor of chemical and petroleum engineering at the University of Southern California Mohammad Sahimi described a 1977 announcement by the State Department that Iran was going to purchase eight nuclear reactors from the US. The two countries signed the US–Iran Nuclear Energy Agreement in July 1978, just months before the overthrow of the shah, to facilitate nuclear energy cooperation and to expedite export and transfer of technology and equipment to Iran's nuclear program. Sahimi reports that according to the memoirs of the shah's close confidant and long-time Imperial Court Minister Asadollah Alam, the shah had envisioned possession of nuclear weapons. And at that time, according to the founder of the Atomic Energy Organization of Iran, the country's scientists did carry out experiments extracting plutonium from spent reactor fuel.[14]

In August 2002, the Iranian opposition military organization known as the Mujahedin el-Khalq (MEK), which had fought for years against the Iranian government while operating in Iraq under the protection of sequential Iraqi governments from Saddam Hussein to the US occupation forces, announced that Iran was much further along in uranium enrichment than had previously been known. Specifically, MEK identified then-undeclared Iranian nuclear facilities in Iran: a centrifuge-based uranium enrichment plant at Natanz and a heavy-water production plant at Arak. The evidence was shaky and the original source unreliable (the MEK had long been designated a terrorist organization by the US and European governments, and many still view them as an unstable cult). But within six months the Bush administration officially accused Iran of building a secret nuclear weapons program. The IAEA initiated six months of inspections in the facilities, and determined that the claim of a covert nuclear program was true. The UN's nuclear inspectors at IAEA criticized Iran for the lack of transparency in reporting the activities, but they did not accuse Iran of any substantive violation of the Non-Proliferation Treaty.[15]

The IAEA's assessment wasn't good enough for the US. In June 2003 the US had refused to rule out a military attack on Iran; in September of that year, while claiming Iran was in fact violating its non-proliferation obligations (thus challenging the IAEA position), Bush agreed to back a European initiative designed to pressure Iran.[16] Tehran suspended its enrichment activities as a goodwill gesture, and accepted the additional, intrusive IAEA inspections demanded by the US and Europe. Following the new inspections, the IAEA again reported there was no evidence Iran was building a nuclear weapon. The US dismissed the IAEA report as "impossible to believe."[17]

Throughout late 2003 and into 2004 the US continued to ratchet up pressure on Europe and other countries. The Bush administration succeeded in getting the IAEA to censure Iran, despite the report denying any evidence of an Iranian nuclear weapons program, and eventually got the issue referred to the Security Council, which, unlike the IAEA, has the power to impose sanctions. In March 2004, the US pressured the Council to pass a resolution condemning Iran for its lack of complete transparency. Later that year, and into 2005, US pressure led both the IAEA and the Security Council to pass resolutions demanding that Iran halt its enrichment activity; the European negotiating team, acceding to US pressure, issued a similar demand. In February 2005 Condoleezza Rice, newly confirmed as secretary of state, stated that a military attack on Iran was not on Washington's agenda "at this point in time."[18] Bush was even more explicit: "This notion that the United States is getting ready to attack Iran is simply ridiculous," he said. "And having said that, all options are on the table."[19]

But the Bush administration was concerned about keeping the increasingly skeptical Europeans onboard the anti-Iran crusade. As a result there was a brief shift in US strategy, as Bush announced the US would back the more nuanced negotiating approach of the EU3 partnership of Germany, France, and the UK. He sweetened the deal a bit further, adding that the US would call off its ten-year-long effort to keep Iran out of the World Trade Organization, and allow Iran to buy US-made parts for its civilian airliner fleet.

By August 2005, however, this brief respite was over, and Bush was already repeating the litany that he would not rule out a military attack on Iran. It was in August that the 2005 National Intelligence Estimate (NIE) would "assess with high confidence that Iran currently is determined to develop nuclear weapons despite its international obligations and international pressure..." The *Washington Post* headlined a front-page article "Iran Is Judged 10 Years From Nuclear Bomb" and until the December 2007 NIE that stated unequivocally that Iran did *not* have a nuclear weapon, it was assumed that the 2005 intelligence document was proof of Iran's dangerous intention and capacity to build a nuclear weapon. (In fact, even the *Post* recognized that the earlier NIE's assessment was far from definitive. It acknowledged that while the NIE referred to "credible indicators that Iran's military is conducting clandestine work," it found "no information linking those projects directly to a nuclear weapons program. What is clear is that Iran, mostly through its energy program, is acquiring and mastering technologies that could be diverted to bombmaking."[20]) But Washington's intense drumbeat of war continued, whipping up fear of an allegedly almost-nuclear-armed Iran.

The Bush administration's belligerent rhetoric escalated, threatening US military strikes on Iran as the only response. It was as if the NIE, theoretically the most credible intelligence available, had provided unequivocal proof of an existing Iranian nuke being readied on the launch pad. And nowhere in the debate was any discussion of Iran's rights and obligations under the Nuclear Non-Proliferation Treaty—let alone any broader discussion of the context of international law and the NPT overall. The big contradiction of the NPT—the 800-pound gorilla that no one mentions—is that every country that enriches uranium to fuel its nuclear power plants has the knowledge to build a nuclear bomb. Because it's the same technology, it just needs to be done more— better, faster, and longer. No other NPT-signatory country is prohibited from enriching all the uranium it wants, building all the nuclear power plants it wants. (Of course many of us wish that the NPT prohibited *all* nuclear power and enrichment—it's *all* too dangerous. But the NPT doesn't do any such thing.) So Washington's fiat, in which Iran is denied the rights it has as an NPT signatory simply because the US doesn't trust its government, represents a breathtaking kind of nuclear double standard. Especially when compared to Washington's quick acquiescence not only to Israel's huge unacknowledged and un-inspected nuclear arsenal, now three decades old, but also to the brazen nuclear weapons testing by India and Pakistan in 1998—all of which were carried out outside the strictures of the NPT and all of which have been quickly accepted, even welcomed, and in the case of India perhaps legalized, by the US.

What about Iran's support for terrorism?

Since the 1979 overthrow of the US-backed shah of Iran, the accusation of Iran being a "state supporter of terrorism" has been a hallmark of US policy. The State Department's *2007 Country Reports on Terrorism* claims that "Iran remained the most active state sponsor of terrorism."[21] But even if all the allegations were true (very uncertain, since no evidence is provided), they would not provide a legitimate basis for US threats, sanctions, or attacks against Iran.

The State Department report claims that

Iranian authorities continued to provide lethal support, including weapons, training, funding, and guidance, to some Iraqi militant groups that target Coalition and Iraqi security forces and Iraqi civilians. In this way, Iranian government forces have been responsible for attacks on Coalition forces. The Islamic Revolutionary Guard Corps (IRGC)-Qods Force, continued to provide Iraqi militants with Iranian-produced advanced rockets, sniper rifles, automatic weapons, mortars that have killed thousands of Coalition and Iraqi Forces, and explosively formed projectiles (EFPs) that have a higher lethality rate than other types of improvised explosive devices (IEDs), and are specially designed to defeat armored vehicles used by Coalition Forces.

The report also states that "Iran remains a threat to regional stability and U.S. interests in the Middle East because of its continued support for violent groups, such as Hamas and Hizballah, and its efforts to undercut the democratic process in Lebanon, where it seeks to build Iran's and Hizballah's influence to the detriment of other Lebanese communities."

There is no evidence and little detail provided, beyond the broad claim that Iran is providing "extensive funding, training, and weapons" to those groups. The report does not acknowledge that both the most important "Palestinian group with leadership in Syria," Hamas, and Hezbollah in Lebanon are important political parties that have been democratically elected to majority and near-majority positions in their respective parliaments. Both, while certainly maintaining military wings, also provide important networks of social services, from clinics and hospitals to schools, daycare centers, food assistance, and financial aid to the impoverished, disempowered, and (in the case of Hamas in Gaza) imprisoned populations of Lebanese and Palestinians. Some of the actions carried out by the military wings of Hamas and Hezbollah have in fact targeted civilians in violation of international law, and thus might qualify as "terrorist" actions. But the majority of their actions have been aimed at illegal Israeli military occupations: of south Lebanon in the case of Hezbollah, and of Gaza and the West Bank in the case of Hamas. The notion that Iran's support for these elected organizations somehow puts it at the top of the list of states supporting terrorism, let alone gives the US the right to attack it, has no legitimacy.

The State Department listing goes on to accuse Iran of pursuing policies in Iraq that appear inconsistent with its own stated objectives regarding stability in Iraq, and inconsistent with the objectives of the Iraqi government and the US-led occupation forces in Iraq. Given the wide disparity of objectives and even definitions between the US view of "stability in Iraq" and the Iranian view, it is hardly surprising that the US might judge Iranian actions, or even its presence (since no actual actions are detailed) as "inconsistent with its stated objectives." But to equate such "inconsistency" with "support for terrorism" requires an enormous stretch.

The Bush administration also accuses Iran's Revolutionary Guard Corps of being "increasingly involved in supplying lethal assistance to Iraqi militant groups, which destabilizes Iraq." It is not clear why the State Department includes that alleged support (for which no evidence has been shown), in their report on "terrorism." The unsubstantiated US claim has consistently been that Iran is providing assistance in the production of "explosively formed penetrator" bombs used against US military patrols in Iraq. The State Department's own definition of terrorism starts with the recognition that it means an attack on noncombatants,[22] which certainly does not apply to wartime military attacks against armed occupation soldiers on patrol.

The State Department report goes on to condemn Iran for remaining "unwilling to bring to justice senior al-Qa'ida (AQ) members it has detained, and has refused to publicly identify those senior members in its custody. Iran has repeatedly resisted numerous calls to transfer custody of its AQ detainees to their countries of origin or third countries for interrogation or trial." Given more than six years of the Bush administration's own "unwillingness to bring to justice senior al-Qaeda members it detained in 2003" and even earlier in Guantánamo, and the US's "refusal to identify publicly these senior members in its custody" and its continued resistance to "numerous calls to transfer custody of its al-Qaeda detainees to their countries of origin or to third countries for interrogation and/or trial" the hypocrisy of claiming this as evidence of support for terrorism is astonishing.

The US has a history of blaming Iran for a host of nefarious deeds, most of the time with little or no evidence to back its claims. This strategy succeeds in portraying Iran as part of what President Bush called the "axis of evil," although it predates the Bush administration. (During the 1993 Oslo negotiations between Israel and the Palestinians, President Clinton reportedly promised Israel that the US would step up efforts to isolate Iran.) In June 2001, Bush's newly installed Justice Department alleged that unnamed Iranians had "inspired, supported, and supervised" the bombing of the US military barracks, Khobar Tower, in Saudi Arabia five years earlier.[23] But according to then Assistant Secretary of State Martin Indyk, "We have not reached the conclusion that the Iranian Government was involved or responsible for the attack."[24]

In 1994, a Jewish community center in Buenos Aires was bombed, resulting in 85 deaths. Claims of Iranian involvement were made by anonymous Clinton administration officials, but never proved; twenty Argentines were acquitted in a long trial in the 1990s. In 2007 a new 800-page indictment was issued by Argentine government prosecutors identifying top Iranian officials allegedly responsible for the bombing. In response, an Argentine judge requested that the international police agency Interpol issue arrest warrants for the named Iranian officials, which Interpol voted to do in November 2007. But even the judge who had made the request admitted to the BBC that "he had no doubt that there was pressure on the Argentine authorities to join in international attempts to isolate the regime in Tehran." And the *Wall Street Journal* reported that the Interpol vote was a result of pressure from the Bush Administration, along with Israeli and Argentine diplomats. And James Cheek, the US ambassador to Argentina at the time of the bombing, admitted that "to my knowledge, there was never any real evidence [of Iranian responsibility]. They never came up with anything."[25]

Is Iran a threat to Israel? What about the other way around?

Israel has been a key player in the US campaign against Iran, both in cheerleading for more intensive US military escalation and in gearing up for the possibility of its own military strike should the US not take what it deemed necessary steps. While Israel and the pro-Israeli lobbies in the US strongly backed the US invasion of Iraq, Israeli security officials and public opinion had long claimed that Iran, not Iraq, represented an existential threat to Israel.[26] Iran, not Iraq, has been a primary target of Israel's constant state of both military and ideological mobilization. On September 8, 2004, Israeli Prime Minister Ariel Sharon said that the international community had not done enough to stop Iran from developing a nuclear weapon and warned that Israel would take its own measures to defend itself. More recently, Israel announced its rejection of the December 2007 US National Intelligence Estimate—which indicated that Iran did not have a nuclear weapons program—less than 24 hours after its release. Iran remained a threat, the Israeli government said, and their mobilization would remain unchanged.

In 2005 the London *Sunday Times* reported that "Israel's armed forces have been ordered by Ariel Sharon, the prime minister, to be ready by the end of March for possible strikes on secret uranium enrichment sites in Iran, military sources have revealed. The order came after Israeli intelligence warned the government that Iran was operating enrichment facilities, believed to be small and concealed in civilian locations."[27] Throughout the 2006–2007 build-up of rhetoric, provocation, sanctions, and threats against Iran by the US, Israel both pushed the US to go further and added its own threats. By January 2007 Israeli Prime Minister Olmert made direct and public threats that Israel might launch a military strike against Iran.[28]

The threats were (and are) not idle. In 1981 Israel carried out a unilateral military attack against Iraq, destroying the half-finished French-built Osirak nuclear power reactor. The action was unanimously condemned internationally, and even President Reagan deemed it illegal. Israel appears to believe it can replicate that attack, this time against Iran—in 2004, Likud Knesset member Ehud Yatom said, "The Iranian nuclear facilities must be destroyed, just as we did the Iraqi reactor." That same year Israel acknowledged it had purchased 500 BLU-109 bunker-buster bombs, using funds from a $319 million US military assistance program. The bombs are designed to penetrate up to seven feet of reinforced concrete and could destroy Iran's specially built underground nuclear power facilities.[29]

The analysts at the authoritative website GlobalSecurity.com asserted that

> It would be difficult for Israel to strike at Iran without American knowledge, since the mission would have to be flown through American [formerly Iraqi] air space. Even if the United States did not actively participate with operations inside Iranian air space, the US would be a passive participant by virtue of allowing Israeli aircraft unhindered passage. In the eyes of the world, it would generally appear to be a joint US–Israeli enterprise, any denials notwithstanding.[30]

And Israel's powerful lobbies in the US have embraced Israel's approach to Iran. By the end of 2007, the influential pro-Israeli think tank the Washington Institute for Near East Policy (WINEP) had issued a report calling for an intensive US–Israeli dialogue on how to respond to what they claim are Iran's nuclear plans, including ways to attack Iran's nuclear facilities.[31] The report was issued weeks after the release of the NIE that expressed the US intelligence agencies' consensus that Iran did not have a nuclear weapons program. In Congress, longstanding pro-Israeli positions among both parties remain a stumbling block to efforts to build coalitions to prevent a US military strike against Iran.

In early June 2008, every major candidate for the US presidential elections, a host of members of Congress, President Bush, Secretary of State Condoleezza Rice, and a raft of other US officials, policymakers, and others came to reassert their support for Israel and vie to be the "most supportive" of Israel at the Washington, DC conference of the powerful pro-Israel lobby group the American–Israel Public Affairs Committee (AIPAC). Virtually all the officials who spoke used the opportunity to escalate their anti-Iran rhetoric. Within days after the conference ended, Israeli politicians also began ratcheting up their rhetoric—perhaps to match that of their US backers, perhaps in anticipation of their own looming electoral fights.

On June 6, in the most explicit threat yet seen from the Israeli government, the Israeli newspaper *Yedioth Ahronoth* reported that Israeli Transportation Minister Shaul Mofaz, a former army chief of staff and former defense minister, had claimed that an Israeli attack on Iranian nuclear sites was "unavoidable" because sanctions had failed to deny Tehran nuclear technology with bomb-making potential. "If Iran continues with its program for developing nuclear weapons, we will attack it. The sanctions are ineffective," he said. "There will be no alternative but to attack Iran in order to stop the Iranian nuclear program." He said that such an attack could only be conducted with US support.[32] (On the next day, the *New York Times* reported that "oil prices had their biggest gains ever on Friday, jumping nearly $11 to a new record above $138 a barrel, after a senior Israeli politician raised the specter of an attack on Iran and the dollar fell sharply against the euro."[33])

Is Iran fomenting a nuclear arms race in the Middle East?

For decades prior to the US–Iran nuclear crisis, real nuclear armament and proliferation in the Middle East have remained a serious problem. While neither Iran nor Iraq possess nuclear weapons or even active nuclear weapons programs, and even putting aside the dangerous nuclear arsenals in the nearby volatile India and Pakistan theater, there was (and is today) a powerful, dangerous, unmonitored, and provocative operational nuclear arsenal in the very center of the Middle East. It belongs not to Iran, but to Israel.

US claims regarding the escalating danger of a nuclear arms race in the Middle East have largely failed to take into account the provocative nature of Israel's unacknowledged but widely known nuclear arsenal of 100–400 high-density nuclear bombs, produced at its Dimona nuclear center in the Negev desert. Israel's nuclear weapon was first tested jointly with apartheid South Africa in 1979; its existence was made public by whistleblower Mordechai Vanunu in 1986. Israel, with US support, maintains a policy of "strategic ambiguity," officially neither confirming nor denying the existence of its nuclear weapons. (This policy was weakened substantially in December 2006, when then Israeli Prime Minister Ehud Olmert publicly named Israel in his list of countries with nuclear weapons.[34])

There is little question that as long as Israel remains the Middle East's sole nuclear power, other countries in the region will continue seeking nuclear parity, particularly while Israel continues to violate international law and provoke its neighbors with its occupation of Palestinian, Lebanese, and Syrian territory. Alternatively, some countries may seek cheaper and more easily hidden chemical or biological weapons of mass destruction, often termed the "poor countries' nuclear weapons."

Egypt, which considered but ultimately abandoned the creation of a nuclear weapons program, signed the non-proliferation treaty in 1980. For more than 25 years Cairo has attempted—so far unsuccessfully—to win support for a nuclear weapons–free zone throughout the Middle East. Israel, with US backing, has opposed it every time. In February 2006, in the IAEA debate that led to the resolution that sent the Iran issue to the Security Council for consideration of sanctions, Egypt and others pressed the US to accept compromise language supporting—sort of—such a nuclear weapons–free zone as the price for keeping the Europeans and most of the non-aligned developing countries on board. The resolution states that solving the Iranian issue would contribute to "realizing the objective of a Middle East free of weapons of mass destruction, including their means of delivery."[35]

The US had resisted this language, claiming Iran might use it in propaganda against Israel. The *New York Times* described how "the Americans backed down and accepted compromise language."[36] But in fact the language was identical to that of a famous UN Security Council decision the US itself had written—Resolution 687, which ended the 1991 Gulf War against Iraq—which said that disarming *Iraq* would be a step "towards the goal of establishing in the Middle East a zone free from weapons of mass destruction and all missiles for their delivery." The US had done nothing to implement that goal, of course; a State Department official involved in the original drafting of 687 said years later that it was never meant to be taken seriously, that it was only included "as a sop to the other countries."[37]

In December 2006 Israeli Prime Minister Ehud Olmert let slip that Israel in fact *did* belong on the list of nuclear weapons states—which he identified as "America, France, Israel and Russia." Whether or not Olmert's statement was intentional, he made it just a few days after Robert Gates, during his confirmation hearings as the Bush administration's new secretary of defense, said that one of the possible motives for Iran's nuclear program was the fact that Israel had nuclear weapons.[38]

What about international law? Is Iran in violation? Is the US?

Under Article IV of the Non-Proliferation Treaty (NPT), Iran as a "non–nuclear weapons state" signatory has the right to produce and use nuclear power for peaceful purposes, including for energy production. Signatories to the NPT that do not have nuclear weapons (all but the US, the UK, France, Russia, and China) agree not to build or obtain nuclear weapons; in return they are promised access to nuclear technology and the right to produce and use nuclear power. Indeed, throughout the 1970s the US pushed the shah of Iran to build nuclear power plants to enable Iran to use more of its abundant oil supplies for export. So Iran's production of nuclear fuel and its construction of nuclear power plants is well within its rights under the NPT. The US-orchestrated decision of the UN Security Council to strip Iran of those rights and impose sanctions if Iran continued to exercise them has no grounding in international law; it is based solely on the US claim that it doesn't trust Iran.

Article VI of the NPT also commits the five nuclear weapons powers to move toward complete nuclear disarmament—and the US and the other four nuclear weapons states all remain in violation of this article. More immediately, the United States is also in violation of the Advisory Opinion of the International Court of Justice, which ruled in 1996 that "*the threat or use of nuclear weapons would generally be contrary to the rules of international law applicable in armed conflict, and in particular the principles and rules of humanitarian law*" (emphasis added).[39] As early as spring 2002, more than a year before the invasion of Iraq, the Bush administration's new Nuclear Posture Review already included military preparations to use nuclear weapons against seven countries, including Iran.[40] (The others were Iraq, China, Russia, Syria, Libya, and North Korea.) That threat and others— more recently through hints and anonymous administration, think-tank, or journalistic sources— stand in clear violation of the International Court of Justice, the UN's highest judicial body. The violation is particularly serious because as a "non–nuclear weapons state" that is a signatory to the NPT, Iran has the right to absolute protection from nuclear attack by the five "official" nuclear-weapons states, including the US.

In addition to its specific nuclear violations, the United States is in violation of the UN Charter and all the principles of international law that prohibit preventive war. The 2002 National Security Strategy (NSS) document reflected the neoconservative goals of global domination and willingness to use preventive attacks to maintain power:

> We must adapt the concept of imminent threat
> to the capabilities and objectives of today's

> adversaries. The greater the threat, the greater is
> the risk of inaction—and the more compelling the
> case for taking anticipatory action to defend
> ourselves, even if uncertainty remains as to the
> time and place of the enemy's attack. To forestall
> or prevent such hostile acts by our adversaries, the
> United States will, if necessary, act preemptively.[41]

In fact, what the 2002 NSS called for was not at all preemptive, but rather the *preventive* use of military force, without even the claim of an imminent threat (generally understood to mean missiles being loaded onto a launch pad or a similarly urgent and immediate danger). It was the same false claim used to justify the invasion of Iraq—there was nothing "preemptive" about it. The war's initial pretext was the claim that Iraq might *someday* possess the means to create a nuclear weapon—which even if true would have remained a purely preventive, and thus illegal, move. As the *Washington Post* reported, the NSS's new military policy would go even beyond legitimating Washington's conventional military force to include, in explicit violation of the NPT, allowing the US to use nuclear weapons preventively against non–nuclear weapons states—such as Iraq and Iran.[42]

What could Iran do in response to a US military strike?

In April 2006 a *New Yorker* article by renowned investigative journalist Seymour Hersh cited key military sources who claimed that the US was already planning a military strike against Iran's underground alleged nuclear sites—using nuclear weapons. Washington officially denied the claim, but did little to tamp down the resulting rise in speculation that a preventive US nuclear strike was in fact under serious consideration, maybe already in preparation. Among members of Congress, even among some committed to ending the war in Iraq and trying to prevent war in Iran, there was a tendency toward a kind of relief that the Bush administration appeared to be considering "only surgical strikes" against Iran, rather than a full-blown invasion. But those same members of Congress acknowledged that they had no idea what level of US escalation—perhaps even including calls for invasion despite troop shortages due to the war in Iraq— might follow Iran's likely retaliation for a US attack.

A wide range of possibilities would be open to Iran. While US officials might call a military attack "only a surgical strike," Iran would certainly call it an act of war—which would indeed be an accurate term. Iran could send troops across its borders to attack US troops in Iraq or shoot missiles into occupied Baghdad's US-controlled Green Zone. Iranian troops could invade and occupy southern Iraq. Iran could attack US troop concentrations in Kuwait, Oman, Qatar, or elsewhere in the region, or go after US ships in Bahrain, home of the Navy's Fifth Fleet. It could attack Israel. It could retaliate against US or allied oil tankers in nearby shipping lanes, and even sink a tanker. It could close the Strait of Hormuz, through which 45 percent of the world's oil passes. The impact on the world economic system would be swift and devastating.

In conventional terms, Iran's military is no match for the US. Iran has faced years of military sanctions, and its military strategy is focused primarily on training troops to defend the homeland against invasion and foreign military occupation. But the assortment of possible retaliatory options for Iran represents only the easy ones, those Iran could carry out with hardly a second thought. Certainly Iran's government might choose to respond to an illegal US or Israeli military strike by non-military means. Tehran might decide to take the moral/political high ground, to respond with a legal challenge in the International Court of Justice or with a request for a special session of the UN Security Council. It might choose not to respond militarily at all.

But while Iran might choose not to respond militarily, a military response is certainly likely, not only because of the wide range of military alternatives it is capable of carrying out, but because Iran in fact would have a legal right to use force against a US attack. Under the terms of Article 51 of the United Nations Charter, Iran has "the inherent right of individual or collective self-defense if an armed attack occurs against a Member of the United Nations, until the Security Council has taken measures necessary to maintain international peace and security." Should the US, Israel, or anyone else launch a preventive attack on Iran's nuclear facilities, that attacking country, not

Iran, would stand in violation of international law and the UN Charter. Article 2, Sections 3 and 4 of the Charter require that "All Members shall settle their international disputes by peaceful means in such a manner that international peace and security, and justice, are not endangered. All Members shall refrain in their international relations from the threat or use of force against the territorial integrity or political independence of any state, or in any other manner inconsistent with the Purposes of the United Nations."

Aside from the feasibility and legality of military strikes and the range of possible responses, the actual effects of a US attack would be devastating. First and most important, huge numbers of Iranians would die. Estimates vary: some of the alleged nuclear facilities are in the midst of cities; other locations are not even publicly known. According to the Pentagon-connected Rand Corporation, "While the US could probably knock out many of the Iranian nuclear facilities using bunker-busting munitions, there would be heavy civilian casualties—probably in the thousands."[43] Another study conducted by Oxford Research Group researcher Paul Rogers compares likely civilian deaths in Iran with those in Iraq:

> The civilian population in that country [Iraq] had three weeks to prepare for war in 2003, giving people the chance to flee potentially dangerous sites. But... attacks on Iranian facilities, most of which are in densely populated areas, would be surprise ones, allowing no time for such

evacuations or other precautions. Military deaths
in this first wave of attacks would be expected to
be in the thousands. Civilian deaths would be in
the many hundreds at least, particularly with the
requirement to target technical support for the
nuclear and missile infrastructure, with many of
the factories being located in urban areas. The
death toll would eventually be much higher if Iran
took retaliatory action and the United States
responded, or if the US took pre-emptive military
action in addition to strikes on nuclear sites.[44]

Politically, there is little doubt that a US or Israeli
military strike on Iran—on nuclear targets or any
other—would also consolidate broad public support
for Iran's nuclear program. While anti-nuclear opinions
and small-scale opposition do exist in Iran, they have
dwindled in the face of US and Israeli threats to Iran's
NPT-guaranteed right to nuclear technology. A strike
would strengthen the most hard-line elements within
Iran's multifaceted diverse polity.

It is certainly possible that Iran would respond to
a US attack without resorting to military force. In
April 2008, there was a terrible explosion at a revered
Shi'a mosque in Shiraz, in which at least twelve
worshipers were killed and more than 200 injured.
Iranian officials vacillated in the following months
between asserting that it was an accident and claiming
that it was a terrorist bombing and that Iran held
Washington responsible for supporting the terrorist
forces that had carried it out. Significantly, Tehran did

not threaten military retaliation, but instead said it
was considering bringing charges against the US in
the International Court of Justice (ICJ), the world
court that has jurisdiction to judge conflicts between
countries.[45] Whether or not either the original
accusation of US involvement or Iran's statement of
intent regarding the ICJ was true, its actions indicate
that Iran does see the multilateral institutions of
international law as potential venues for dealing with
its grievances. That viewpoint, of course, is not shared
in Washington. To the contrary, earlier efforts to hold
the US accountable in the ICJ for violations of
international law (such as charges brought by
Nicaragua in the 1980s regarding US responsibility
for mining harbors and other attacks on civilian
targets) led to a US rejection of the ICJ's jurisdiction
even to hear the case.

PART II

A SHORT HISTORY OF RECENT

US—IRAN RELATIONS

Wasn't Iran once an ally of the US?

US involvement in Iran has a long history, beginning back in the 1920s when the US collaborated with Great Britain to exploit Iran's vast oil riches. (See "Where does oil fit into US policy toward Iran?") In 1951, Great Britain and the US faced the possibility of losing control of Iran's oil when the democratically elected Prime Minister Mohammed Mossadegh announced his intention to nationalize his country's key natural resource.

In response, in 1953 the CIA orchestrated a coup that overthrew Prime Minister Mossadegh, and installed Mohammed Reza Pahlavi on the throne as the shah of Iran, backing his claim to absolute power. The shah immediately set about consolidating a vast apparatus of repression, torture, and control, centered in the SAVAK secret police and bolstered by uncritical and unlimited US military and police assistance. In return, the shah reversed Mossadegh's nationalization policies and put in place an arrangement in which Iran's oil industry and its profits would be shared with a new consortium of US and British oil companies. For the next 25 years the shah of Iran would serve, alongside Israel, as one of the key pillars of US strategy in the Middle East. The people of Iran, who faced widespread assassination, arrest, torture, and denial of virtually all political rights, would pay the price.

For example, in 1963 the shah announced his "White Revolution," a package of US-backed pro-

Western privatization and other economic reforms. The new economic policies were devastating to Iran's population, particularly the working class and the poor. Protests and strikes resulted. One of the largest of that year's many uprisings erupted in response to the arrest and imprisonment of one of the leaders of the religious sector of the anti-shah mobilization, the Ayatollah Ruhollah Khomeini, then still living in Iran. When he was released eighteen months later, Khomeini broadened his critique of the shah to oppose the US directly; soon after, the shah forced Khomeini into exile in Iraq, where he spent most of the next fifteen years.

During that time, a huge anti-shah movement took shape across Iran, led by forces as diverse as the conservative Islamist clerical supporters of Ayatollah Khomeini, to the communist-led oil workers' unions, to the wide array of leftist Iranian student organizations. By January 1978, labor strikes and huge demonstrations against the escalating human rights violations—arrests, torture, and executions were common—brought a majority of the Iranian people into motion against the shah's regime. The shah's backers in Washington were getting very worried. In the summer of that year, despite reports by other officials that the shah was collapsing and that some kind of revolution was unstoppable, then National Security Advisor Zbigniew Brzezinski and Energy Secretary James Schlesinger were continuing to tell the shah that the US would provide military support, and

Brzezinski was still advocating direct US intervention to "stabilize" Iran.[46] President Carter opposed military intervention, but it was unclear what the US could do as its strategic ally collapsed. In September, after the shah declared martial law, a month-long oil workers' strike largely paralyzed the country.

It was clearly too late for any US intervention. On January 16, 1979, the shah fled, first to Egypt and later to several other countries. On February 1, 1979, Khomeini returned home to a tumultuous welcome in the streets of Tehran.

What happened after the US-backed shah was overthrown?

The shah's army, once armed and trained by the US, quickly made clear that it would not challenge the anti-shah guerrillas and popular forces in the street, and the military's neutrality brought about the final collapse of the shah's regime. By April 1979 a national referendum was held, in which Iranians approved the transformation of their country into an Islamic republic to be based on a theocratic governing system led by a religious Council of Guardians. And just as quickly, the collaboration between Islamist and leftist political forces deteriorated, as Khomeini's regime consolidated its rule based on a harsh interpretation of Islam that left little room for progressive secular influence. The students and workers that had played such key roles in the anti-shah mobilization were sidelined, many facing renewed repression under the new regime.

In the meantime, the Carter administration was faced with increasing demands from the deposed shah of Iran to come to the US for medical treatment. After frantic US diplomatic efforts failed to find him refuge somewhere else, the shah was welcomed to the US in October 1979.

Regardless of his illness, many Iranians believed the shah's entry into the US presaged a US campaign to return him to power, and it was largely in outraged response that Iranian student militants occupied the US embassy in Tehran on November 4, 1979, in what would become the famous hostage ordeal. Fifty-two US diplomats and others in the embassy were taken captive and held for 444 days. They were released just after the new President Ronald Reagan was inaugurated on January 20, 1981. President Jimmy Carter's inability to secure the hostages' release— particularly the events surrounding the deaths of eight US soldiers in a failed helicopter rescue effort in April 1980—was widely viewed as the critical factor in his losing reelection in November 1980. The Carter administration carried out the negotiations that led to the hostages' release, and in the Algiers Agreement that codified the arrangements the US agreed it would not intervene in the internal affairs of Iran and would lift its trade sanctions and assets freeze against Iran. But the timing of the actual release—only minutes after Reagan repeated the oath of office—was interpreted as a deliberate slap against President Carter, and the opening to the new Reagan administration may have set the stage for its engagement with Iran in the years following, including in what became known as the "Iran—Contra affair," the covert and illegal arms sales to Tehran carried out by Reagan administration operatives throughout the mid-1980s to gain cash for the Nicaraguan Contras.

The US lifted the earlier sanctions as required under the Algiers Agreement, but the Reagan administration reimposed the sanctions in 1984, and they have remained in place, continuing to create economic problems for Iranians today.

US policy has consistently claimed the "right" to control strategic resources, especially oil, across the globe. In his January 1980 State of the Union address, President Jimmy Carter made clear that he deemed Persian Gulf—including Iranian—oil part of "the vital interests of the United States of America," and that any attack on that oil "will be repelled by any means necessary, including military force."[47] This was at the height of the Cold War and following the Soviet invasion of Afghanistan, and Carter was referring primarily to a threat to US hegemony from the Soviet Union. But the implications of his policy extended far beyond Afghanistan to the rest of the region.

After the overthrow of the shah in 1979, Iran emerged as a key target of the new "Carter Doctrine," which took shape following the Soviet invasion of

Afghanistan that same year. In the same State of the Union speech in which Carter threatened military force to maintain control of Persian Gulf oil, he announced the creation of a Rapid Deployment Force and the opening of new military bases prepared for action in the Persian Gulf area. He also called for reinstatement of mandatory military draft registration for eighteen-year-old men.

When Iraq invaded Iran in September 1980, beginning the long Iran–Iraq war, the disastrous situation presented a new opportunity for US policymakers. The two countries in the Middle East with the greatest potential capacity to challenge US hegemony in the region were now at war with each other—spending their national treasure, killing each others' young men in the hundreds of thousands, and strategically weakening each other. The US moved quickly to weigh in on the side of Iraq, the weaker party, with the goal of keeping the fighting going for as long as possible and maintaining US power in the region. The Reagan administration also secretly sold arms to Iran (in the Iran–Contra scandal), but the main US military and financial backing went to Iraq, and the US was seen around the world as backing Saddam Hussein's regime in Baghdad.

The US pressured the UN Security Council to issue its first call for a ceasefire while Iraqi troops under Saddam Hussein still occupied huge swathes of Iranian territory in the first week of the Iraqi invasion of Iran. In 1984, Iraq tried to expand the conflict, including by attacking Iranian ships. In response, Iran's navy began to threaten the oil tankers of Kuwait and other Gulf countries supporting Iraq as they traveled in the Gulf.

The US's direct military involvement in the war escalated further when President Reagan ordered that the Kuwaiti tankers be re-flagged as American ships, and sent US Navy warships out to protect them from any potential Iranian attack. In July 1988 the US warship *Vincennes* on patrol in the Persian Gulf (having skirmished with Iranian gunboats inside Iran's territorial waters earlier that day) shot down an Iranian Airbus passenger plane, killing all 290 people, including 66 children, on board. The US first claimed that the crew of the *Vincennes* mistook the giant passenger plane for an F-14 fighter jet. But the claim could not be defended, and eventually the US paid compensation to Iran, although it never officially apologized.

The end of the Iran–Iraq war in 1988 did not bring any change in the hostile US relations with Iran. The US's direct military involvement on Iraq's side in the Iran–Iraq War was understood in Iran and throughout the region as consistent with the anti-Iran antagonism which had characterized US–Iranian relations since the overthrow of the shah and the triumph of the Islamic revolution—with no official diplomatic relations and continuing US-imposed economic sanctions against Iran.

What was Iran's connection to "Desert Storm," the 1991 US war on Iraq?

Having chosen its side, Washington continued its supportive partnership with Saddam Hussein after the end of the Iran–Iraq war, but ended it two years later in August 1990 when Iraq invaded Kuwait. That reversal of the US–Iraqi alliance was sudden and, for many, unexpected. In July 1990, just a week before the invasion, in what would be her last meeting with Saddam Hussein, US Ambassador April Glaspie gave Saddam Hussein what amounted to a yellow "caution" light regarding the invasion of Kuwait, telling the Iraqi president that "we have no opinion on the Arab–Arab conflicts, like your border disagreement with Kuwait."[48] But despite its ambiguous approach to the escalating Iraq–Kuwait tensions and the clear, imminent threat of war, Washington used Iraq's attack on Kuwait as a pretext to launch a global crusade aimed at reasserting US superpower status even as the Soviet Union collapsed and the Cold War sputtered to an end.

After years of a close US–Iraq alliance, Iraq and especially Saddam Hussein personally (who had, after all, brutally repressed his population throughout that alliance with the US showing no concern) were suddenly demonized and targeted for a new US war, launched in the name of the United Nations.

Iraq was the new target, and Saddam Hussein quickly replaced Ayatollah Khomeini as the bad guy of choice. George H.W. Bush's National Security

Directive 54, issued on January 15, 1991 on the eve of his launching Operation Desert Storm, focused primarily on Iraq. But like the Carter Doctrine a decade earlier, it had broader regional implications, and Iran would not be spared. Iran's oil, as well as its potential regional influence and power, remained as challenges to the US determination to maintain domination and control of the strategic Persian Gulf region. NSD 54 opened with the words: "Access to Persian Gulf oil and the security of key friendly states in the area are vital to US national security. Consistent with NSD 26 of October 2, 1989, and NSD 45 of August 20, 1990, and as a matter of long-standing policy, the United States remains committed to defending its vital interests in the region, if necessary through the use of military force, against any power with interests inimical to our own."[49] Iran was as much a potential target as Iraq.

In 1996, without providing any evidence, the US accused Iran of involvement in the bombing of the US military's Khobar Tower barracks in Saudi Arabia. A month after the bombing, Congress extended the existing economic sanctions against Iran for an additional five years. The US sanctions against Iran were never as devastating to ordinary people as the international economic boycott the US orchestrated against Iraq in 1990—not least because they remained unilateral, and Iran maintained relatively normal economic relations with the rest of the world. But even sanctions by one country can have a damaging impact, when that one country is the biggest player in the world economy and every other country is concerned about maintaining good relations with it. Additionally, after decades of US support for Iran under the shah, virtually all of Iran's infrastructure, including its civilian air fleet, much of its tele-communications and other infrastructure, as well as much of its military hardware, were US-manu-factured and US-controlled—meaning that Iran's ability to purchase airplane parts or telephone system components from France wouldn't do much good when the systems they had to repair were from factories in Ohio.

Not surprisingly, as the sanctions hit the civilian population they strengthened public opposition to US policies and the US government even among those Iranians who might otherwise favor cultural ties and international openness, including with Americans. (It should be noted that the US sanctions were not uniformly implemented. Vice President and former Halliburton CEO Dick Cheney acknowledged during the 2000 election campaign that despite the sanctions Halliburton had continued to do "business with Libya and Iran through foreign subsidiaries."[50])

How has the US been dealing with Iran since September 11 and the Iraq war?

After the terrorist attacks of September 11, 2001, Iran became a major partner in the US invasion and occupation of Afghanistan. Iran had long opposed the Taliban government in Afghanistan, both for sectarian religious reasons (the Taliban enforced a rigid version of Sunni Islam, while Iran is adamantly Shi'a) and because Tehran was concerned about instability on its eastern border. So Iran emerged as a major participant in the US-led multilateral coalition that took control of Afghanistan after the overthrow of the government, including the international and UN-backed campaign to create a new Afghan government under US occupation. US diplomats worked closely with their Iranian counterparts within and outside UN frameworks and spoke admiringly of their commitment and collaborative approach to Afghanistan diplomacy. (See "Is diplomacy possible between the US and Iran?")

That cooperation, however, was apparently not enough to satisfy the Bush administration. Just a few weeks after the inauguration of the US-backed Hamid Karzai as president of occupied Afghanistan, something Iran had helped make possible, Bush delivered his 2002 State of the Union address, in which he targeted Iran as part of the so-called axis of evil. Less than a year later, Bush suspended all bilateral contacts with Iran.

The US-led coalition invaded Iraq in March 2003, and US efforts to isolate Iran escalated dramatically as the occupation of Iraq ground on. In February 2006, after two years of lobbying against Iran in the International Atomic Energy Agency (IAEA), the

UN's nuclear watchdog and the agency responsible for reviewing such issues, the US succeeded in convincing its allies to send the issue of Iran's nuclear power program to the Security Council, with the goal of imposing harsh new international sanctions against Iran. In response, Iran announced it was ending its voluntary special cooperation with the IAEA, a program of rigorous, intrusive inspections Tehran had agreed to for several years in hope of easing pressure from the US.[51]

Once the issue of Iran's nuclear program had shifted to the Security Council, the US, backed by the UK, France, and Germany and with reluctant acquiescence from Russia and China, imposed new demands on Iran, insisting that it stop enriching uranium altogether, despite its rights under the Non-Proliferation Treaty. When Iran refused to abandon its right to nuclear power, the US and its allies orchestrated two sets of economic sanctions against Iran. While the specific measures were directed toward individuals and institutions allegedly tied to Iran's nuclear enrichment efforts, the real goal was less about punishing individuals than it was about provoking Tehran and increasing overall pressure on Iran.

The Bush administration has never addressed Iran's legal right under the NPT to produce its own fuel for peaceful nuclear power. Instead it has simply claimed it doesn't trust Iran and therefore can forcibly prevent Iran's exercise of its right.

And the US continued to ratchet up pressure on Iran. By August 2007 Bush was claiming that Iran's "pursuit of technology *that could lead to nuclear weapons* threatens to put [the Middle East] *under the shadow of a nuclear holocaust*" (emphasis added). The US would, Bush threatened, "confront this danger before it is too late."[52] This rhetoric was particularly dangerous because it was chillingly reminiscent of the orchestrated public statements of 2002, in which the president, vice president, and secretary of state all invoked the false threat of an Iraqi nuclear attack—the infamous "we don't want the smoking gun to be a mushroom cloud" remark[53] threatening war against Iraq—a nation that, like Iran, had no nuclear weapons program. That time the US had made good on their threat. The question hovered whether they would do it again.

Bush faced a continuing drop in support at home for the war in Iraq and was preparing for the long-expected report of Iraq commander General David Petraeus and Ambassador to Iraq Chester Crocker, to be delivered in September 2007. Despite the so-called surge that had begun earlier that year, Iraq remained in crisis, and the White House decided to shift the blame for the Iraqi failure to Iran, specifically to President Mahmoud Ahmadinejad. Bush accused Ahmadinejad of supporting Shi'a resistance forces in Iraq through both training and weapons supplies, and said: "Iran has long been a source of trouble in the region. Iran's active pursuit of technology that could lead to nuclear weapons threatens to put a region already known for instability and violence under the shadow of a nuclear holocaust." He went on to reaffirm his commitment to "regime change," claiming that what was needed was "an Iran whose government is accountable to its people, instead of to leaders who promote terror and pursue the technology that could be used to develop nuclear weapons." Ahmadinejad responded with heated rhetoric of his own, saying that US influence in the region was collapsing so fast a power vacuum was coming soon. "Of course, we are prepared to fill the gap," he said.[54]

The difference, of course, was that Ahmadinejad, while perhaps rhetorically accurate vis-à-vis US failures in Iraq, did not threaten to attack the United States. In fact, on his own the Iranian president could not threaten to attack the US, Israel, or any other country. Unlike the power-sharing arrangements of the US Constitution, Iran's president is not the commander in chief of the military and does not control its mission. Instead, according to Article 110(4) of Iran's Constitution, the "supreme leader" of the powerful clergy holds "supreme command of the armed forces." The supreme leader also has the power, according to Article 110 (5), to declare war and peace and mobilize the armed forces.[55] Throughout Ahmadinejad's presidency the supreme leader has been Ayatollah Ali Khamenei, who supports the president but is far from uncritical of Ahmadinejad. Given the well-known disagreements with Ahmadinejad among Iran's

powerful elites, his offensive rhetoric has little to back
it up.

US efforts to provoke Iran continued throughout
2007 and beyond. The navy increased the number of
US aircraft carrier groups and destroyers in the
Persian Gulf. US minesweepers were sent to the
Strait of Hormuz. In January 2007 US troops in
northern Iraq kidnapped five Iranian diplomats
working at the request of the US-backed Iraqi
government, holding them in violation of their
diplomatic immunity. In fall 2006, Bush gave his Iraq
commanders explicit orders to kill or capture Iranians
in Iraq.[56]

In February 2007 US officials in Baghdad
trumpeted that they had proof Iran had provided Iraqi
insurgents with weapons that had been used to kill
US troops. No evidence was provided. General Peter
Pace, then chairman of the Joint Chiefs of Staff,
denied the accusation against Iran. Just a day after
high-level US military officials in Baghdad claimed
that the "highest levels" in Iran were directing attacks
on US troops in Iraq, Pace pulled back: "I would not
say by what I know that the Iranian government
clearly knows or is complicit," he said on February
12, 2007.[57]

A month later, while the UN Security Council
was again debating whether to escalate the sanctions
against Iran, British military personnel on patrol in
the Persian Gulf engaged in what the British Defense
Ministry called "routine boarding operations of

merchant shipping in Iraqi territorial waters." The inspection regime, ostensibly designed to protect Iraqi oil terminals and go after what CBS News described as "smugglers, insurgents and terrorists,"[58] was carried out under the terms of a UN Security Council mandate. But the British patrol ship was operating in the Shaatt al-Arab waterway, which divides Iran and Iraq, and which is difficult to navigate in the best of times. These were not the best of times. Fifteen British sailors and marines were taken into custody by the Iranian navy, and held under the accusation of having been operating illegally in Iranian territorial waters. After two weeks, the British troops were released unharmed. There was speculation that the Iranian move may have been tied to growing frustration in Tehran with the US's detention of five Iranian diplomats, whom US soldiers had seized in early January in the northern Iraqi city of Irbil and had been holding ever since, even though the diplomats had been operating under the Iraqi government's authorization. What was indisputable was that neither the British nor Iranian governments attempted to ratchet up the volatile situation any further. Fear grew that in the case of a similar incident involving US troops, Washington would not hesitate to turn a controllable situation into a full-blown crisis—with incalculable military consequences.

In August US troops arrested seven more Iranian civilians, this time in Baghdad (though that group was released the next morning with an "apology" from US

General Petraeus). Construction began on a large new US military base in Iraq less than five miles from the Iranian border.[59] And US pressure on its allies began to pay off. In September, French foreign minister Bernard Kouchner, former humanitarian activist and founder of Médecins sans Frontières (Doctors Without Borders), warned that the world must prepare for war to oppose Iran's nuclear program.[60] The newly elected president of France, Nicolas Sarkozy, soon joined the Bush administration and his own foreign minister in calling the Iranian nuclear issue the worst crisis in the world, and calling for more pressure on Iran to "enable us to escape an alternative that I say is catastrophic: the Iranian bomb or the bombing of Iran."[61]

In January 2008, when Bush made his first visit to Israel and the Palestinian territories, he again used the moment to increase pressure on Iran. Bush's trip was officially designated as a follow up on the failed Annapolis Israeli–Palestinian peace conference of the previous month, but the real (and only half-heartedly hidden) agenda had far less to do with Israel–Palestine than with Iran. Bush administration officials stated the trip's goals included the need to "clarify any confusion" regarding the US position on Iran. In other words, the need to "clarify" that the NIE's recognition that Iran did not have a nuclear weapons program would not mean an end to US threats against Iran.

Just 48 hours before Bush left for the Middle

East, the high-profile but low-substance "incident" involving the Iranian speed boats in the Strait of Hormuz took place (see page 55). Among the White House officials weighing in on the seriousness of the "incident" was press secretary Dana Perino, who asserted that the boats' action "was not normal behavior." Asked whether the incident would "bolster [the president's] intent to go over there and rally support against Iran," Perino said it was "just another point of reference for people in the region who are concerned about the behavior of Iran."[62]

So if Iran doesn't have nuclear weapons, what is the US really so worried about?

US concern about Iran—and resulting efforts to either buy its allegiance, ensure its weakness, or destroy its military and economic capacity—did not begin with the unilateralist, militarist extremism of the George W. Bush administration. Certainly Iran's massive oil reserves make it of interest to all countries dependent on imports of foreign oil to maintain advanced industrial societies. But there are other reasons too, for Iran's centrality in US strategic planning.

Historically, Iran and Iraq were the only two countries in the Middle East with all the prerequisites to become indigenous regional powers: water, oil, and size. Water made them self-sufficient, oil provided wealth, and the size of land and population guaranteed the possibility of power. It is also not coincidental that

Iran and Iraq are two of only three Middle Eastern countries (the other being Egypt) with long histories as independent nation-states. With a few border adjustments (Kuwait was once part of Iraq, Iraqi Kurdistan a more recent inclusion) the modern nations—and peoples—of Iraq and Iran grounded their histories and identities in the ancient countries of Mesopotamia and Persia respectively.

For this reason the United States viewed the 1980–1988 Iran–Iraq war as a boon, a means of seriously weakening both potential regional challengers. In 1980, Iran's neighbor and long-time competitor Iraq, led by President Saddam Hussein, eyed the new Islamist government next door, saw what appeared to be weakness, and invaded. For the US, the Iran–Iraq war, which would ultimately last eight years and cost nearly a million lives, provided a strategic opportunity. Wanting both sides to lose— or at least to maintain the damaging combat as long as possible—the US weighed in largely on the side of what appeared to be the weaker of the two, Iraq. US economic and military assistance included satellite technology to help Saddam Hussein's military direct its chemical weapons, and provision of the germs for Baghdad's (later) much-feared biological weapons program. The human toll on both sides was enormous, but Iran's losses were particularly staggering, as it sent much of a generation of young men—and eventually old men, young boys, and some women—by the tens of thousands in human waves

straight into better-armed Iraqi positions. But despite
its losses in the war with Iraq, Iran would soon surpass
its long-time opponent. When Iraq collapsed as an
independent country, following its defeat in the 1991
Gulf War, twelve years of crippling sanctions, and the
2003 US invasion and occupation, Iran reemerged as
the only potential regional challenge to Washington's
domination.

So the claimed US fears and resulting media
frenzy over a potentially nuclear Iran must be viewed
in the context of far more longstanding US concerns
over Iran's decades-long efforts, similar to those of so
many countries, to weaken its potential competitors
and consolidate its own power and influence in the
Middle East. One component of that US concern has
to do with economic power and influence; certainly
today the struggling US economy provides a strong
motivation for unease regarding Iran, which continues
to challenge the preeminence of the US dollar in the
crucial global oil markets.

Writing in August 2005, oil economist William
Clark described what he anticipated would be the US
response to Iran's planned creation of a new oil
trading market, or bourse, then anticipated for 2006.
He wrote that while the official rationale for any US
attack on Iran

> will be premised as a consequence of Iran's
> nuclear ambitions, there are again unspoken
> macroeconomic drivers underlying the second
> stage of petrodollar warfare—Iran's upcoming

oil bourse. ... In essence, Iran is about to commit a far greater "offense" than Saddam Hussein's conversion to the euro for Iraq's oil exports in the fall of 2000. Beginning in March 2006, the Tehran government has plans to begin competing with New York's NYMEX and London's IPE with respect to international oil trades—using a euro-based international oil-trading mechanism. The proposed Iranian oil bourse signifies that without some sort of US intervention, the euro is going to establish a firm foothold in the international oil trade. Given US debt levels and the stated neoconservative project of US global domination, Tehran's objective constitutes an obvious encroachment on dollar supremacy in the crucial international oil market.[63]

Although the launch of the Iran oil bourse was delayed several times, Iran did succeed in eliminating reliance on the dollar for its oil sales. In March 2007 Japan agreed to purchase Iranian oil with yen, and by September China accepted Iran's request to purchase its crude with euros. By December 2007, as reported by the Russian press agency RIA Novosti, "Iran has stopped selling its oil for US dollars, the Iranian ISNA news agency said on Saturday... 'In line with a policy of selling crude oil in currencies other than the US dollar, the sale of our country's oil in US dollars has been completely eliminated,' ISNA reported Oil Minister Gholamhossein Nozari as saying. He also said 'the dollar is no longer a reliable currency.'"[64]

Even while hiding its economic concerns, by 2006 the Bush administration was no longer publicly relying solely on claims that Iran was building a nuclear weapon as the basis for its threats. The 2006 edition of the National Security Strategy document repeated the 2002 version's aggressive language in support of preventive war, but then focused more directly on other non-nuclear allegations against Iran:

> the Iranian regime sponsors terrorism; threatens Israel; seeks to thwart Middle East peace; disrupts democracy in Iraq; and denies the aspirations of its people for freedom. The nuclear issue and our other concerns can ultimately be resolved only if the Iranian regime makes the strategic decision to change these policies, open up its political system, and afford freedom to its people. This is the ultimate goal of US policy. In the interim, we will continue to take *all necessary measures* to protect our national and economic security against the adverse effects of their bad conduct.[65]

Again, the US was threatening direct force against Iran in the short term.

Where does oil fit into US policy toward Iran?

Oil has always been central to US relations with Iran, despite the US ban on purchasing Iranian oil since 1979. For a global power such as the US, the issue is not so much direct access to Iran's oil; the US doesn't need to import that much Iranian or indeed Middle Eastern oil in general for its own use. Far more important is maintaining control of Iran's and other countries' oil supplies: the ability to determine price and the quantity available, and to guarantee access to oil to favored friends and deny it to competitors.

Historically, it was Britain, before the US, who moved to control Iran's oil. According to analyst Antonia Juhasz,

> Having no oil of their own, the British had 'gone global' more rapidly than the Americans, having laid claim to the oil of Iran, then Persia, in 1908. Persia's vast oil wealth formed the basis of the Anglo-Persian Oil Company, later called the Anglo-Iranian Oil Company, and later still British Petroleum, then BP. At the outset of World War I, Winston Churchill, then First Lord of the Admiralty of the British Navy, railed against the monopoly power of the world's oil corporations. To overcome the control exercised by the oil companies, Churchill argued, the British government would have to get into the oil business itself. As he told the Parliament, 'We must become the owners, or at any rate the controllers, at the source of at least a proportion of the supply of natural oil which we require.' The Parliament agreed, and in 1914 the British government became majority owner of the Anglo-Persian Oil Company.[66]

US oil companies became involved some years later, and from the beginning control of oil was understood as having political as well as economic advantages for Washington. In the early 1950s when

Iran's Prime Minister Mohammed Mossadegh moved toward nationalization of Iran's oil, Britain—heavily dependent on Iranian oil and still recovering from the devastation of World War II—was desperate for help from the US. In response, the CIA orchestrated the overthrow of the democratically elected Mossadegh in 1953 and installed the newly created shah of Iran. The State Department announced that "in the cause of defense and in the fight against communism, the five sisters [US oil companies] must be brought to Iran."[67]

Despite the repressive and unpopular shah's dependency on the US for military and political support, Iran joined the OPEC cartel in 1960 and was part of the oil embargo of the early 1970s. When the shah was overthrown and the Islamic Republic of Iran established in 1979, Iran's oil was nationalized once again, and quickly embargoed by the US, although the US oil companies were still benefiting from the higher oil prices then in place around the world.

The crusade to gain control of strategic resources, especially oil, remains a hallmark of the so-called global war on terror, the Bush administration's banner covering its wars in Afghanistan and Iraq, attacks on Somalia and expansion of military bases across the Middle East. Antonia Juhasz notes:

> Under the rubric of the Global War on Terror, the Bush administration has implemented the greatest realignment of US forces since the end of the Cold War. One needs only a map of Big Oil's overseas operations, the world's remaining

oil reserves, and oil transport routes to track the realignment and predict future deployments of the U.S. military. The greatest reserves of oil in the world are found in the Middle East. Accordingly, since taking office, the Bush administration has opened new U.S. military bases and installations in Iraq, Qatar, Kuwait, Turkey, Afghanistan, Pakistan, and a major U.S. naval base at Diego Garcia in the Indian Ocean. A contract for a new base has been signed with Djibouti, situated to the north of Somalia across the Red Sea from Saudi Arabia. The U.S. maintains military installations in Egypt, the UAE and Oman. As former Bush White House Speech writer David Frum wrote in 2003, 'the war on terror' was designed to 'bring a new stability to the most vicious and violent quadrant of the Earth—and new prosperity to us all, by securing the world's largest pool of oil.'[68]

While Iraq was the first strategic target in the Bush administration's post–September 11 "war on terror," it was not the only target. With the destruction of Iraq's oil infrastructure in the US invasion and occupation, and 2008's skyrocketing $140+ per barrel cost of oil, reclaiming control over the oil industry remains a crucial goal for US powerbrokers and policymakers. A decade before 9/11, Paul Wolfowitz—Bush's future undersecretary of defense—outlined what would be the neo-conservative policy toward Iraq, Iran, and maybe other petro-states: "In the Middle East and Southwest

Asia, our overall objective is to remain the predominant outside power in the region and preserve US and Western access to the region's oil."[69]

What does Iran have to do with the US war on Iraq?

The 2003 US invasion of Iraq, the overthrow of Saddam Hussein's Ba'athist government, and the dissolution of the Iraqi army greatly empowered Iran, by removing the most significant impediment to its quest for regional hegemony. Both Iran and Iraq had oil wealth, water, and large populations—the requisites to become indigenous powers. The two countries had historically competed to win supremacy in the Middle East, most directly and devastatingly in the Iran—Iraq war of the 1980s. The US occupation of Iraq not only destroyed that country's potential, but enabled Iran's emergence as the region's greatest indigenous power.

General David Petraeus and Ambassador Ryan Crocker's September 11, 2007 report on Iraq to Congress had two goals for the Bush administration. One was to shore up public support for the "surge," the 30,000 additional troops that had brought the US occupation force up to 165,000 (plus about 150,000 US-paid mercenaries). The claim that the "surge" was working was presented as "good news." But beyond the "good" news, Petraeus described the counter-balancing "troubling" news: it is increasingly apparent, he said, that Iran is trying to "fight a proxy war against the Iraqi state and coalition forces in Iraq." In answer to a reporter's query, Petraeus denied that his speech was designed to ratchet up pressure against Iran. But there was no question that demonizing Iran was a central aim of the report. Secretary of State Condoleezza Rice joined the campaign, calling Iran "a very troublesome neighbor," and her deputy, John Negroponte, weighed in with unsubstantiated allegations that Iran was providing arms to the resurgent Taliban in Afghanistan.

Petraeus's hearing was designed to fit carefully into the administration's existing anti-Iran crusade. Vice President Cheney was reported to have already proposed launching air strikes at suspected training camps in Iraq supposedly run by Iran. In the months leading up to Petraeus's appearance before Congress, a series of Iraq-based military reports blamed Iran for a variety of consequences of the illegal US occupation. In July, Brigadier General Kevin Bergner, a spokesman for the US occupation troops in Iraq, said members of Iran's Quds force had helped plan a January attack in the holy Shi'a city of Karbala, in which five US troops died.[70] But the specificity of his allegations was not backed up by any specific evidence.

By the middle of 2007, claims of Iran's "meddling" in Iraq already had become central to Washington's build-up against Iran. This rising focus on Iran and particularly the allegations of its involvement in Iraq were becoming serious concerns for the US-backed Iraqi government. Despite the massive death and destruction caused by the Iran–Iraq war, the two countries share not only a long border but an ancient shared history. The war caused enormous suffering, and inevitably strong antagonisms in both countries, but those longstanding ties appear to remain. Certainly there were always many differences—Iranian Persians speak a different language than Iraqi Arabs, the cultures vary in many ways—but there are many similarities as well. Both are modern countries that trace their roots to the earliest histories of humanity in Mesopotamia and the ancient Persian empires. Both are cosmopolitan and multicultural societies with large and diverse ethnic, linguistic, and religious minorities of which the Kurds are only the largest. And aside from the broad ties between the two countries, many Iraqi Shi'a, particularly in the southern part of the country, hold longstanding and deep political as well as personal ties to Iran. Many top officials in Iraq's parliament and government spent their years of exile in Iran during Saddam Hussein's regime, and many had married Iranians. The prominent Iraqi cleric Ayatollah Ali al-Sistani, who was actually born in Iran, remains perhaps the most influential voice among Iraqi Shi'a, particularly in southern Iraq, and has maintained close ties to Tehran throughout the years of the US invasion and occupation of Iraq. In mid-2007, in what was widely seen as a shift away from Iran and toward a more overtly Iraqi national identity, the political party with which Sistani is most closely identified, SCIRI

(Supreme Council of the Islamic Revolution in Iraq), changed its name to the Supreme Islamic Iraqi Council. But the party remains simultaneously closely allied with Iran and influential within the US-backed Iraqi government, and Sistani is respected throughout Iraq.

In August 2007, a senior Iraqi official in Baghdad reported that his government received regular US intelligence briefings about suspected Iranian activities. He worried that the US was "becoming more focused on Iranian influence inside Iraq," he said. "And we don't want Iraq to become a zone of conflict between Iran and the U.S."[71]

But Iraq already is part of that "zone of conflict." In a clearly provocative move, the US announced in September 2007 that it was beginning construction on the newest US military base in Iraq, to be built less than five miles from the Iranian border.[72] US officials often claim, without evidence, that Iran is leading a rising "Shi'a crescent" that threatens the stability of Arab regimes across the Middle East, but there is no doubt that Iran is actually very concerned about the violence and instability in Iraq and the permanent US military deployment on its western border. In fact, with the US occupation of Iraq and the US-dominated NATO occupation of Afghanistan, as well as a massive US troop deployment in Turkey and US special forces operating not-so-secretly in Pakistan, Iran remains largely surrounded by US and allied military troops.

After the December 2007 release of the National Intelligence Estimate that found that Iran did not have a nuclear weapons program, many in the Middle East, even Arab leaders who had been longstanding clients of Washington began to distance themselves from the Bush administration's anti-Iran crusade.

In February 2008 Iranian President Ahmadinejad paid a state visit to Baghdad, the first Iranian president to enter Iraq since the Iran–Iraq war ended twenty years before. Although clearly major security arrangements were in place, Ahmadinejad's drive from the airport to Baghdad and other cities, his seemingly leisurely strolls through markets and into mosques, were deliberately orchestrated to contrast with the high-security secrecy that characterized all of Bush's brief visits to Iraq, where he huddled in a US military base for a few hours and scurried out. Even pro-government (and thus pro-US) UAE newspapers described how

> Iranian President Mahmoud Ahmadinejad appeared happy and proud during his recent visit to Iraq. It was clearly harvest time for the president, whose visit marked the success of Iran's strategy in the previous five years. Ahmadinejad was the first president, other than US President George W. Bush, to visit Iraq since the US invasion, but the visits of the two presidents could not have been more different. While Bush's three visits to the country were kept secret, the Iranian president's visit was highly publicised. He arrived in Baghdad and toured the city openly. … Ahmadinejad had a message, which is that politics and strategy can

achieve much more than war. His visit to Iraq successfully conveyed his message, and achieved what could not be achieved through an eight-year war between Iraq and Iran that claimed the lives of more than a million people, caused over $1 trillion in losses to the economies of both countries and left behind a legacy of destruction. The visit also established the growing Iranian influence in Iraq… [and] confirms beyond doubt that Iran is the most effective player among Iraq's neighbours. [73]

Aside from sectarian and broader regional affinities, Iran's $2 billion annual trade with Iraq was likely part of the reason for the popularity of Ahmadinejad's tour. The Iranian president's visit also represented a serious challenge to US control of the Iraqi government, reminding Washington that while the officials may have been elected under the protection of the US occupation, many of them have even longer-standing ties to Tehran. Washington has not yet recognized that reality. As it ends the US occupation of Iraq—which remains an urgent necessity—the US will have to come to terms with the close ties between the two nations and the fact that Iran will be involved in and with Iraq in the future.

PART III

ALTERNATIVES TO WAR

Who opposes an attack on Iran? What are the alternatives to such an attack?

It is certainly not surprising that virtually all Iranians oppose a US military strike on Iran. But perhaps more unexpected is that the vast majority of the American people do not support any attack on Iran. In a June 2008 poll, more than half of the respondents (57 percent) said that diplomacy was "the one best way" to deal with the current situation with Iran. Only a little more than a quarter said that trying to impose international sanctions was the best way, and, crucially, only 7 percent of Americans chose military action. Significantly, the poll shows that even during the escalation of anti-Iran rhetoric, provocations, and propaganda that occurred between fall 2007 and spring 2008, the American people were not convinced. Support for sanctions, doing nothing, military threats, and military attacks all dropped, and only support for diplomacy rose—from 35 percent to 57 percent.[74]

The Bush administration claims that its aggression toward Iran is partly based on concerns about human rights violations there. But Iranian human rights activists whom the Bush administration would like to claim as its supporters in fact stand firmly opposed to a US military strike, perhaps most prominently Shirin Ebadi, the Iranian lawyer, feminist, and former judge, and winner of the 2003 Nobel Peace Prize. In a 2005 *New York Times* op-ed, "The Human Rights Case against Attacking Iran," Ebadi argued that "for human rights defenders in Iran, the possibility of a foreign military attack on their country represents an utter disaster for their cause." Describing Iran's vibrant though vulnerable human rights movements, Ebadi went on: "Independent organizations are essential for fostering the culture of human rights in Iran. But the threat of foreign military intervention will provide a powerful excuse for authoritarian elements to uproot these groups and put an end to their growth... In 1980, after Saddam Hussein invaded Iran and inflamed nationalist passions, Iranian authorities used such arguments to suppress dissidents." She recognized that "American hypocrisy doesn't help, either. Given the longstanding willingness of the American government to overlook abuses of human rights, particularly women's rights, by close allies in the Middle East like Saudi Arabia, it is hard not to see the Bush administration's focus on human rights violations in Iran as a cloak for its larger strategic interests." Ebadi's conclusion was very clear: "Getting the Iranian government to abide by these international standards is the human rights movement's highest goal; foreign military intervention in Iran is the surest way to harm us and keep that goal out of reach."[75]

Ebadi's and other human rights defenders' opposition to US military attack or intervention is particularly important because human rights violations in Iran remain a serious concern. As in the United States, some of the worst abuses focus on the death penalty: imposition of the death penalty against children, execution through cruel means, and more. Iran has issued a standing invitation to the UN's human rights agencies, and six UN delegations have visited the country, but human rights activists are concerned about Iran's failure to implement their recommendations. In June 2008 Ebadi and several international human rights organizations, noting that failure, appealed to Iran to cooperate with the UN Human Rights Council in addressing ongoing abuses, including the death penalty issues, death in detention, punishment by flogging and amputation, mistreatment of human rights defenders including denial of their right to travel, repression of women, students, and labor activists, and more. The lack of freedom of expression in Iran, including in the press, remains a grave concern as well. The activists also called on Iran to provide the now-overdue reports it promised to the UN Human Rights Committee and the UN Committee on Economic, Social, and Cultural Rights. As Ebadi said, "cooperation with the United Nations on human rights is crucial to help the Iranian government to improve respect for international human rights standards binding upon the Islamic Republic."[76]

In January 2007, Mohamed ElBaradei, head of the UN's nuclear watchdog agency, the IAEA, said, "I still believe that the only solution to the Iranian issue—which is in our hands right now—is dialogue, is negotiation, is engagement by the neighbors and by all the relevant parties. The Arab countries have to be engaged, the U.S. has to be engaged. We need to try that. We need to invest in peace because the alternative is not there, and the alternatives could be 10 times worse."[77] Nine months later he reiterated that force should be a last resort in Iran, and urged people not to forget the lessons of the Iraq war. Condoleezza Rice criticized ElBaradei for urging caution.[78]

ElBaradei's colleague Hans Blix, who headed the UN's search for WMDs in Iraq before the US invasion and now chairs the Weapons of Mass Destruction Commission in Sweden, took a similar position, saying that Iran is not a threat and that Bush was overreacting: "There's time to negotiate with Iran and to carry out those negotiations in a sensible manner. I think they use too much sticks and they should use more carrots, just as they've done in the case of North Korea, where they are making some headway."[79]

Among political elites in the US, a group of influential former secretaries of state came together in March 2008 to call for direct talks with Iran. While not explicitly rejecting the "military option," they called for the US to "open a line of dialogue with Iran, each saying it was important to maintain contact with adversaries and allies alike." The group was led by Bush's own former secretary of state Colin Powell, and included Nixon advisor Henry Kissinger, George H.W. Bush's top diplomat James Baker, and Madeleine Albright and Warren Christopher from the Clinton era.[80] Speaking to the Israeli newspaper *Haaretz*, former President Jimmy Carter called on the Bush administration to initiate direct talks with the Iranian regime to resolve the issue of Tehran's nuclear program. He said "the best option was dialogue with Iran."[81] And even conservative supporters of the Iraq war, who show little concern about Iranian casualties, have spoken out against expanding the war to Iran. According to James Carafano of the right-wing Heritage Foundation, "There are no good military options.... When you're trying to stabilize Iraq and you've got this long border between Iran and Iraq, and you're trying to keep the Iranians from interfering in Iraq so you can get the Iraq government up and running, you shouldn't be picking a war with the Iranians. It just doesn't make any sense from a geopolitical standpoint."[82]

Numerous military figures have warned against the danger of a US attack on Iran. Those willing to go public include Colin Powell's former chief of staff at the State Department, Colonel Lawrence Wilkerson, and Lieutenant General Robert Gard, former president of the National Defense University. Retired Army General and former head of Central Command John Abizaid said, "Iran is not a suicide nation... I doubt that the Iranians intend to attack us with a nuclear weapon. I believe that we have the power to deter Iran, should it become nuclear. War, in the state-to-state sense, in that part of the region would be devastating for everybody, and we should avoid it—in my mind—to every extent that we can."[83] General Wesley Clark joined the centrist VoteVets organization in February 2007 to create an online "Stop Iran War" petition. Speaking of US–Iran talks, Clark asked, "could not such a dialogue, properly conducted, begin a process that could, over time, help realign hardened attitudes and polarizing views within the region? And isn't it easier to undertake such a dialogue now, before more die, and more martyrs are created to feed extremist passions?"[84] Other military critics of a strike on Iran include Admiral William Fallon, the chief of Central Command, whose resignation in March 2008 sparked new fears of a possible US attack (see "With so much opposition, is it still possible the US will attack Iran?").

Most of the high-ranking military critics have retired from active-duty service; while there are indications that there is wide opposition to a strike on Iran across the top ranks of the military, few active-duty generals have been willing to take the perceived political or career risk of warning against potential presidential decisions—however disastrous—while still in the service. But by mid-2008, a few high-ranking active-duty military officials—particularly though not exclusively from the navy—were starting to hint at more critical positions. Vice Admiral Kevin Cosgriff, commander of the US Fifth Fleet and thus the highest ranking US naval commander in the Middle East, told ABC News that a war with Iran would be "pretty disastrous," and there would be "echoes and aftershocks" throughout the region. He said the ideal way to relate to Iran would be through diplomatic methods. "Nobody I've spoken to suggests that going to war with Iran is a good thing," he said.

"The preferred path by far is the diplomatic path, keep working with the international community to bring the right sort of pressure to bear on the Islamic Republic of Iran."[85]

Cosgriff and others have been calling for greater contact with Iran, even if not entirely rejecting the use of military force. Cosgriff said that contact between the navies of the US and Iran would be beneficial, similar to contacts that existed between the US and Soviet navies during the Cold War. Admiral Fallon, who had resigned apparently in protest of the Bush administration's war threats, had made such a call even earlier. Bush administration officials reported that during his tenure as head of Central Command, Fallon had proposed a similar navy-to-navy relationship with Iran as a way of starting a dialogue with the country after almost thirty years without diplomatic relations. The idea was "quickly rejected" by the White House, which claimed it would be "rewarding" Tehran. "In the conduct of daily business we routinely have excellent communications with the Iranian Navy," Admiral Fallon said. "When the conditions are right it might be a reasonable way of interaction—to build on existing maritime communications." He declined to discuss the specific initiative, though he did say that the navy could provide a way to begin a process of resuming some level of relations with Iran.[86]

At the same time even Bush's own defense secretary, Robert Gates, began to shift his language to a more nuanced, less rigid tone regarding dialogue with Iran—significant because his new approach seemed to contradict both the White House and the campaign rhetoric of 2008 Republican presidential nominee Senator John McCain.

And retired Marine General Anthony Zinni, former head of Central Command, agreed on the need to prevent "unintended confrontations" with Iran. He proposed a naval coordination center across the Persian Gulf area, with bridge-to-bridge communications and search and rescue coordination between US, Iranian, and all the regional Arab navies. "These could be a starting basis, with more co-operation along the lines of Admiral Cosgriff's caveat leading to greater connections," General Zinni said. Admiral Cosgriff, in the meantime, acknowledged that people "have this unsettled feeling... people are inclined to think something," regarding the possibility of a US attack on Iran in 2008. But he dismissed the reports as "urban legend."[87]

In its effort to mobilize Middle Eastern and global support for escalating pressure against Iran, the Bush administration has routinely claimed that Arab governments are "afraid" of Iran, that the "Sunni Arab allies of the US" are threatened by the Shi'a Iranian government. In fact, while Arab regimes long backed by the US do indeed see Iran as a regional contender for economic and political influence, challenging their own long-time regional strategic protector in Washington, there is much greater fear of the consequences of a US–Iran military clash. In January

2007 the secretary-general of the Arab League, Egyptian diplomat Amr Moussa, told the gathering of wealthy and powerful at the World Economic Forum in Davos, that any US military strike against Iran would "backfire" and that Washington should use dialogue to resolve the tensions with Iran as well as the violence in Iraq.[88]

Unlike the run-up to the invasion of Iraq, when the Bush administration succeeded in coercing dozens of countries into at least nominal membership in its coalition, in the case of Iran, no country other than Israel is prepared to unequivocally back the White House. Some governments, including France and the UK, refuse to reject a US military attack absolutely, but have not backed the Bush administration's overt calls to consider military strikes. While the European—especially British and French—governments focus on escalating sanctions against Iran, public opinion in both those countries remains even more strongly against US militarism against Iran than it was in the run-up to the US invasion of Iraq. And of course the failure of the Iraq war provides ever more grist for the mill of global public opposition to a similar—or much worse—debacle in Iran.

Do US sanctions against Iran work? What are the costs?

Sanctions and isolation of Iran were Washington's strategy throughout the 1990s. Shortly after Bill Clinton took office in 1993 he announced a strategy of "dual containment," aimed at suppressing the reconstitution of power in both Iran and Iraq. In 1995, Clinton imposed harsh unilateral trade sanctions against Iran and pressured US trade partners not to engage with Iran. In 1996, Congress passed the Iran–Libya Sanctions Act, prohibiting significant investments in oil or gas projects in either nation.

Although the US sanctions against Iran were not nearly as extreme as those the US imposed on Iraq in the name of the United Nations, the Iranian people still have paid a steep price. Much of Iran's infrastructure—particularly its oil infrastructure and civilian airlines—was created during the shah's regime, so most spare parts required are of US make and thus unavailable under the sanctions. In June 2005, a report prepared for the International Civil Air Aviation Organization "warned that US sanctions against Iran were placing civilian lives in danger by denying Iranian aviation necessary spare parts and aircraft repair.... It said that the U.S. government and major U.S. companies were ignoring international treaties and taking actions that put passengers on Iranian commercial airlines at risk, including thousands of people from other countries traveling to and from Iran." The report pointed to US companies that refused to provide spare parts, seized engines sent to other countries for repair, and even threatened to hold necessary parts for European airlines hostage if those airlines did maintenance work on Iranian planes. The report went on, "The lack of concern for aviation safety is surprising in intensity and vigor." Six months later, a US-made Iranian military transport plane crashed, killing 108 people.[89]

According to the *Los Angeles Times*:

Economic sanctions imposed on Iran by the Security Council and countries such as the United States so far have had few concrete restrictions but have created an atmosphere that makes investors fearful, observers said. "Sanctions are like icebergs," said Saeed Leylaz, an Iranian economist and journalist. "Only 10 percent of the effect is directly attributable to the Security Council. Ninety percent is fear of the U.S." Some officials dread a repeat in Iran of the events in Iraq after the 1991 Persian Gulf War, when sanctions discouraged companies from doing business with Iraqis, whittling at livelihoods of the people while strengthening the hand of Hussein and his inner circle. "Even if something is not on a list, a lot of companies will say, 'Dealing with Iran—oh, I'd better not do it,'" said a European diplomat in Tehran. "It's becoming like 1990s Iraq, when companies used to refuse to sell papers and pencil to Iraq."[90]

When imposed by the biggest economy in the world, "unilateral" sanctions invariably take a multilateral toll, since other countries and financial institutions are eager to stay on Washington's good side. Even so-called smart sanctions, designed only to target those tied directly to Iran's nuclear industry, end up affecting large numbers of people. Designating Iran's entire Revolutionary Guard Corps as a "terrorist entity," as the Bush administration did in late 2007, imposes sanctions on tens or perhaps hundreds of thousands of Iranians whose family members have ties to that huge bureaucracy within Iran's official military.

Oil sanctions diminish Iran's ability to rebuild and improve its seriously eroded oil-refining capacity, thus reducing the amount of gasoline and other oil-based products available for domestic use. And, ironically, the sanctions themselves cause more Iranians to believe that their country needs nuclear power, despite its massive oil reserves, because of the sanctions-driven shortages of refined oil-based fuels.

By the end of July 2006, US pressure on its European allies as well as Russia and China was sufficient to force the Security Council to pass Resolution 1696, which simply ignored Iran's rights as guaranteed under the NPT, and demanded that it "suspend all enrichment-related and reprocessing activities, including research and development." The resolution threatened Iran with more economic sanctions if it refused to stop its activities. The vote was fourteen in favor, only one against—Qatar, the only Middle Eastern country on the council. (In a non-public report just a month later, IAEA Director-General and the prior year's Nobel Peace Laureate Mohamed ElBaradei made clear that Iran was *not* reprocessing uranium.[91])

Immediately after the vote, the US began its campaign to convince and coerce other Council members that another new sanctions resolution should be imposed on Iran if it continued to reject the Council's demand to stop its enrichment activities. The Bush administration succeeded on December 23, 2006: the Council imposed sanctions prohibiting the import into Iran of any nuclear material for its power reactors, and froze the assets outside the country of a number of people and institutions allegedly involved in proliferation activities.

In 2007, ElBaradei called for a "time-out" on Iran's nuclear program, proposing that the UN Security Council suspend sanctions if Iran froze its nuclear program. He also called for direct negotiations, telling CNN that "the key to the Iranian issue is a direct engagement between Iran and the U.S."[92] Instead, the White House kept up the pressure. In March 2007 the Security Council imposed another set of sanctions, which froze the assets of a much larger group of Iranian individuals and institutions, and banned the sales of all Iranian weapons to any other countries.

Contradicting the Bush administration's stance in the Security Council, in December 2007 the US General Accounting Office released a report entitled "Iran Sanctions: Impact in Furthering U.S. Objectives Is Unclear and Should Be Reviewed," which found that "Iran's global trade ties and leading role in energy production make it difficult for the United States to isolate Iran and pressure it to reduce proliferation and support for terrorism. For example, Iran's overall trade with the world has grown since the U.S. imposed sanctions."[93]

But by February 2008, a third US-driven sanctions resolution was under discussion by the key Security Council members. France joined the US to push for a tougher set of sanctions; China and Russia continued to resist, but the UK moved into the debate to bridge the gap between the two sides, and the discussion continued. Given that the US's own intelligence agencies had determined that Iran did not have a nuclear weapons program, and that a new IAEA report had indicated that Iran was cooperating and IAEA inspectors just needed a bit more time to finish their work, several Council members, including China and Russia and even Washington's European allies balked. In response, the US had to soften the harsh sanctions it had originally proposed, and the resolution that was actually passed had little substance. All the travel restrictions and freezing of international assets of Iranians allegedly involved in nuclear weapons–related or other activities the US didn't like were made voluntary—the sanctions would be only a recommendation for each country to implement or not. They would have little additional economic impact on Iran.

The resolution had a symbolic significance, however, as a further broadening of Washington's effort to isolate Iran from the international community. And it had one important political/ strategic component. Article 11 of the new sanctions resolution 1803

Calls upon all States, in accordance with their national legal authorities and legislation and consistent with international law, in particular the law of the sea and relevant international civil aviation agreements, to inspect the cargoes to and from Iran, of aircraft and vessels, at their airports and seaports, owned or operated by Iran Air Cargo and Islamic Republic of Iran Shipping Line, provided there are reasonable grounds to believe that the aircraft or vessel is transporting goods prohibited under this resolution or resolution 1737 (2006) or resolution 1747 (2007)…

Although the overall sanctions language made implementation voluntary rather than mandatory for UN members, that particular language essentially authorized the US to carry out stop-and-search actions of Iranian ships and planes, under cover of a UN Security Council resolution.

South Africa's ambassador to the UN, Doumisani Kumalo, criticized this provision, saying that it "could spark confrontation and further threaten international peace and security."[94]

But such views were ignored. The US and its allies kept the pressure on the Non-Aligned countries—South Africa, Libya, and Indonesia—who were still committed to opposing the resolution. They recognized that even if the new sanctions resolution passed without their support, its symbolic importance would be diminished if they could deny the US a unanimous vote. The vote was scheduled for a Friday, then delayed for the weekend. French

President Sarkozy took on Washington's heavy diplomatic lifting to win support for the sanctions resolution in Pretoria, Tripoli, and Jakarta. When the council reconvened on Monday morning, March 3, reluctant and embarrassed diplomats had been given new orders. The vote was fourteen in favor, zero opposed. South Africa and Libya supported the resolution, and only Indonesia abstained. None claimed that imposing new sanctions would somehow help to prevent war. None of these once resolute Non-Aligned stalwarts tried to claim Iran represented a threat to their national security. To the contrary, each of them had maintained strong South–South relations with Iran for years. What threats were made, what fears forced once-defiant governments to give in to US and French and perhaps other European pressure remains uncertain.

What false claims has the Bush administration made about Iran?

On the nuclear weapons issue, it is false to claim that Iran is violating the Non-Proliferation Treaty by enriching uranium for its nuclear power plants. The NPT (Article IV) allows every country that signs on as a non–nuclear weapons state, including Iran, the inalienable right "to develop research, production and use of nuclear energy for peaceful purposes without discrimination." Further, the treaty actually encourages its signatories to spread the development of nuclear power, and states explicitly that all its signatories "have the right to participate in the fullest possible exchange of equipment, materials *and scientific and technological information* for the peaceful uses of nuclear energy" (emphasis added). So much for Iran breaking the law through knowledge. The NPT's enforcement agency, the International Atomic Energy Agency, has consistently reported that it has no evidence of Iran diverting nuclear materials or programs to military purposes. While the IAEA has been concerned about insufficient transparency in some of Iran's reports, that does not constitute a violation of the NPT. (Iran has rejected the Security Council's demand that it halt all nuclear enrichment activities; those resolutions themselves stand in contradiction to the guaranteed right to produce nuclear power that is central to the Non-Proliferation Treaty.)

It is false to claim that Iran is responsible for the deaths of US troops in Iraq. There is no question that Iranians—businesspeople, diplomats, aid workers, others—are operating in Iraq; they share a long border and a longer history. But there has been no direct evidence—only assertions—presented to back up the claim that the Iranian government has provided Iraqi militias with "explosively formed penetrators" (EFPs) or any other weapons. Andrew Cockburn, in the *Los Angeles Times*, wrote:

> President Bush has now definitively stated that bombs known as explosively formed penetrators—EFPs, which have proved especially deadly for US troops in Iraq—are

made in Iran and exported to Iraq. But in November, US troops raiding a Baghdad machine shop came across a pile of copper disks, 5 inches in diameter, stamped out as part of what was clearly an ongoing order. This ominous discovery, unreported until now, makes it clear that Iraqi insurgents have no need to rely on Iran as the source of EFPs. The truth is that EFPs are simple to make for anyone who knows how to do it.[95]

Indeed, even a *New York Times* article on the same discovery titled "U.S. Displays Bomb Parts Said to Be Made in Iran" acknowledged the uncertainty. "[W]hile the find gave experts much more information on the makings of the E.F.P.'s, which the American military has repeatedly argued must originate in Iran," the *Times* said,

> the cache also included items that appeared to cloud the issue. Among the confusing elements were cardboard boxes of the gray plastic PVC tubes used to make the canisters. The boxes appeared to contain shipments of tubes directly from factories in the Middle East, none of them in Iran. One box said in English that the tubes inside had been made in the United Arab Emirates and another said, in Arabic, 'plastic made in Haditha,' a restive Sunni town on the Euphrates River in Iraq.[96]

Another set of false claims concern Iranian President Ahmadinejad. Certainly much of his rhetoric, clearly designed to bolster his populist domestic base, has been inflammatory and offensive—particularly his questioning of the reality of the Nazi Holocaust. (He has also become well known for his remark at Columbia University denying that there are homosexuals in Iran—although this appeared to be a one-off reference, not part of his ordinary discourse, it is still horrifyingly homophobic, as well as preposterous.) But instead of criticizing the real outrages, US political and media figures have made exaggerated and false claims to rebut and created straw men to knock down. So rather than challenging Ahmadinejad's actual stated hope that Israel's regime, meaning a Jewish-Zionist state occupying Jerusalem, would collapse, the claim was made and repeated unchallenged in the media that he had threatened to "wipe Israel off the map." In this context, US warnings that Ahmadinejad was a madman desperately trying to build a nuclear weapon to attack Israel were especially dangerous. And dangerously false, because under the Iranian constitution the president is not the commander in chief; the chief of the clerical leadership council, not the president, controls the military. It has been widely understood that Ahmadinejad has the backing of the powerful clerical leadership, in particular the supreme leader, Ali Khameini, but that backing is not unequivocal or unchangeable. Indeed there have been numerous occasions in which other individuals close to Khameini expressed opinions challenging Ahmad-inejad, and there are frequent rumors that the selection of former nuclear negotiator Ali Larijani to serve as speaker of the Iranian parliament may signal a shift in official conservative support away from Ahmadinejad.

And a final false claim—the assertion that "the Iranian people" are somehow eager for US sanctions, US efforts at "regime change," perhaps even US military strikes, is a fiction whose failure in Iraq should have made its reassertion vis-à-vis Iran impossible. Certainly there is plenty of opposition to Ahmadinejad and to many of the Iranian regime's policies within civil society and among the Iranian people. But overwhelmingly the domestic Iranian opposition has resisted Washington's pressure to support US militarism toward Iran, has rebuffed offers of financial and/or political "support" from the US, has rejected Iranian exiles (the son of the last shah, among others) who attempt to gain US or other international backing to "return" to power à la Ahmad Chalabi in Iraq, and has made absolutely clear its opposition to any threatened US military attack on its country.

With so much opposition, is it still possible the US will attack Iran?

Many believed that when the December 2007 National Intelligence Estimate confirmed that Iran did not have a nuclear weapons program, the Bush administration no longer had any basis for threatening to attack Iran.

But instead, in the days and weeks after the release of the NIE, the administration and its allies attacked its findings and attempted to maintain the legitimacy of their threats toward Iran. Sen. John Ensign (R-NV) announced legislation that would create a commission to get a "fresh set of eyes" on the NIE's findings. Israeli Defense Minister Ehud Barak restated his opposition to Iran's nuclear production and said, "In our opinion [Iran] has apparently continued that program." And *Newsweek* reported that during his meeting with Israeli Prime Minister Ehud Olmert in January 2008 Bush "told the Israelis that he can't control what the intelligence community says, but that [the NIE's] conclusions don't reflect his own views" about Iran's nuclear weapons program.[97]

It is certainly possible that Bush's reassurance to Olmert reflected a quiet commitment to back an Israeli strike on Iran—Israeli Deputy Prime Minister Shimon Peres said in March 2008 that Israel would not *unilaterally* attack Iran, but he said nothing about an attack backed by the US. Certainly Israel would need at least US permission, if not direct involvement, because an Israeli strike on Iran would have to go through US-controlled (Iraqi) airspace. As reported in *U.S. News and World Report* in March 2008:

> Israel's airstrike deep in Syria last October was reported to have targeted a nuclear-related facility, but details have remained sketchy and some experts have been skeptical that Syria had a covert nuclear program. An alternative scenario floating in Israel and Lebanon is that the real purpose of the strike was to force Syria to switch on the

targeting electronics for newly received Russian anti-aircraft defenses. The location of the strike is seen as on a likely flight path to Iran (also crossing the friendly Kurdish-controlled Northern Iraq), and knowing the electronic signatures of the defensive systems is necessary to reduce the risks for warplanes heading to targets in Iran.[98]

That underlying assessment had actually been made months earlier, by the noted journalist Seymour Hersh. Citing a high-ranking US intelligent official, Hersh wrote in the *New Yorker* that

> America's involvement in the Israeli raid dated back months earlier, and was linked to the Administration's planning for a possible air war against Iran. Last summer, the Defense Intelligence Agency came to believe that Syria was installing a new Russian-supplied radar-and-air-defense system that was similar to the radar complexes in Iran. Entering Syrian airspace would trigger those defenses and expose them to Israeli and American exploitation, yielding valuable information about their capabilities. Vice-President Dick Cheney supported the idea of overflights, the former senior intelligence official said, because "it would stick it to Syria and show that we're serious about Iran." (The Vice-President's office declined to comment.)[99]

And as Bush started his final year in office, he outlined a continuation of his policies and rhetoric toward Iran in his January 2008 State of the Union speech. Despite the findings of the NIE, he proclaimed:

We're also standing against the forces of extremism embodied by the regime in Tehran. Iran's rulers oppress a good and talented people. And wherever freedom advances in the Middle East, it seems the Iranian regime is there to oppose it. Iran is funding and training militia groups in Iraq, supporting Hezbollah terrorists in Lebanon, and backing Hamas's efforts to undermine peace in the Holy Land. Tehran is also developing ballistic missiles of increasing range, and continues to develop its capability to enrich uranium, which could be used to create a nuclear weapon.

Both Bush and Cheney kept up the drumbeat for war. On March 24, 2008 Cheney accused Iran of trying to create weapons-grade enriched uranium, despite the fact that this claim contradicted both the NIE and the most recent report of the IAEA, which had come to the opposite conclusion. Speaking of Iran, Cheney told an ABC interviewer, "Obviously, they're also heavily involved in trying to develop nuclear weapons enrichment, the enrichment of uranium to weapons grade levels."[100] Bush went even further, making up the completely false claim that Iran had "declared" its intention to build and use a nuclear weapon. He told the US-supported Farsi-language Radio Farda that Iran's leaders have "declared they want to have a nuclear weapon to destroy people."[101]

On the same day, US military guards aboard the *Global Patriot*, a US Navy–contracted merchant ship in the Suez Canal, shot and killed an Egyptian merchant selling cigarettes and other goods from a small motorboat to the crews of ships crossing the canal. The brother of the man killed by the navy guards said that the merchants in small boats know not to approach military ships. But "the Global Patriot looked like an ordinary freighter," the brother said. In an ominous reminder, the navy's spokeswoman said that such navy-contracted cargo ships "follow the same rules of engagement as American warships" in responding to approaching boats.[102] Given that Commander Lydia Robertson speaks for the entire US Navy Fifth Fleet, based in Bahrain, directly across the Persian Gulf from Iran, it was hard to miss the unspoken threat of what might happen in the Strait of Hormuz if a US ship that "looked like an ordinary freighter" was approached by a boatload of Iranian cigarette and snack sellers. Would that give the Bush administration a Tonkin Gulf–style pretext for war?

Two months after Bush's State of the Union speech, and also in March 2008, Admiral William Fallon resigned from his position as chief of the US Central Command. His tenure, which had lasted just under a year, had put him in charge of Pentagon activity across a huge swathe of territory from Egypt and Sudan to Somalia and Yemen, across the Middle East to Pakistan and Central Asia, including the key war zones of Iraq and Afghanistan—and Iran. Fallon had publicly opposed the Bush administration's 2007 "surge" strategy in Iraq and supported earlier withdrawal of US occupation troops, and had been known as an outspoken (by military standards) critic of White House and other references to possible military strikes against Iran. He told al-Jazeera "this constant drumbeat of conflict... is not helpful and not useful. I expect that there will be no war, and that is what we ought to be working for."[103] After an admiring profile in *Esquire* magazine described him as the "good cop" to a Bush/Cheney "bad cop" in threatening Iran, he resigned.

Fallon's public position when he resigned was "I don't believe there have ever been any differences about the objectives of our policy in the Central Command area of responsibility."[104] But of course "objectives" are easy—peace, stability, democracy, etc. What he did not deny was the differences he appeared to have with the strategy to achieve those objectives. It remains uncertain whether Fallon chose to resign because he disagreed with the policy or was pushed out for the same reason, but clearly his departure removed a serious impediment to continuing US military threats and, more dangerously, perhaps even military action against Iran.

When Fallon broke his silence three months later, he indicated that he does indeed favor dialogue and patience, not war, with Iran. As the *International Herald Tribune* described it, "he defends his public statements on Iran that stress diplomacy over the use of force. 'People tend to look at things in black and white—we're going to love Iran or attack Iran,' he said. 'That is a very simplistic way to approach a complex problem.'"[105]

The main counterbalance to the president is Congress, but that institution has largely remained unwilling or afraid to challenge the very real possibility of an illegal preventive US military strike against Iran. Some members of Congress have introduced resolutions aimed at ensuring that no military strike could occur without congressional approval, but in general opposition is thin, and in the case of either a real or false provocation, Congress would most likely agree to back a military "response." Israel's consistent drumbeat demanding military force against Iran, and the cheerleading for that position from Israel's powerful lobbies in the US, make it very difficult for senators and representatives even to consider rejecting a US military strike against Iran. Few in Congress, the media, or other policymakers fully understand the danger of a large-scale escalation, up to and including the possibility of ground troop involvement, in response to a likely Iranian retaliation after a US "surgical strike."

While there are differences between the two parties, and Democratic candidate Barack Obama would be less likely to launch an attack against Iran, he would be unlikely to reverse any existing military assault already underway when he took office. Iran was a central issue throughout the campaign season for the 2008 presidential election. Republican candidate John McCain trumpeted his support for military attacks on Iran, on one occasion answering a reporter's question with his own lyrics, sung to the

tune of the 1960s Beachboys hit "Barbara Ann"—
"Bomb bomb bomb, Bomb bomb Iran…" There was
no apology. Democratic nominee Barack Obama and
early frontrunner Hillary Clinton both insisted that "the
military option" against Iran must "remain on the table."
Obama differed from his Democratic rival in his
commitment to offer direct and unconditional
negotiations with Iran if he were president, but both
maintained the position that the US had the right to use
all forms of coercion—up to and including a military
strike—to force Iran to accept Washington's demands.

Some opponents of a military attack on Iran have
vacillated between positions more and less supportive
of such a strike. Henry Kissinger signed on to the
March 2008 statement calling for diplomatic
engagement with Iran (see page 75). But six months
earlier in a *Washington Post* op-ed of his own he wrote:

> Cooperation is possible and should be
> encouraged with an Iran that pursues stability
> and cooperation. Such an Iran has legitimate
> aspirations that need to be respected. But an Iran
> that practices subversion and seeks regional
> hegemony—which appears to be the current
> trend—must be faced with lines it will not be
> permitted to cross: The industrial nations cannot
> accept radical forces dominating a region on
> which their economies depend, and the
> acquisition of nuclear weapons by Iran is
> incompatible with international security.[106]

So according to Kissinger, cooperation with Iran could be imagined as long as Tehran's policy matched Washington's views of stability and cooperation. But in the real world, the US "cannot accept" Iranian influence over a region whose oil makes it so vital to Western capitalist economies.

When the Bush administration began ratcheting up its anti-Iran rhetoric in early 2004, many believed European opposition to a military strike against Iran would emerge as a key impediment to another instance of reckless US military adventurism. But many European governments, including some strongly opposed to using military force against Iran, seem to believe that after the Iraq debacle, a unilateral US military strike on Iran is virtually impossible. They appear convinced that "even the Bush administration isn't that stupid," and so are not pressuring or mobilizing against such a policy, in fact acceding to US pressure for tougher Security Council sanctions. They do not seem to realize that while Bush, Cheney, and some of their closest advisors may not be stupid, many of them are driven by an extremist ideology of unilateralism and militarism that renders irrelevant all other strategic consequences. This rejection of real facts on the ground, in favor of the fanciful beliefs that people across the Middle East are eager for US invasions to impose "regime change" and US-style "democratization" on their countries and that every global problem or economic challenge is best resolved through military force, combined represent a serious danger of reckless military aggression that Europe ignores at its peril.

In November 2004 Europe—led by the UK, France, and Germany—offered new trade deals with Iran in return for its agreement to suspend its nuclear enrichment program. Iran agreed. But when trade talks began the following January, the E-3 raised their price, now demanding a permanent halt in Iran's enrichment activities. By 2006, the UK and France were fully in line with the Bush administration's strategy. That spring the European Union foreign policy chief, Javier Solana, issued a deadline to Iran, saying that it had until the Group of Eight summit planned for summer 2006 to respond to the demand for a permanent halt to enrichment, or the EU would join the US in going to the Security Council. When Iran still refused, Europe made good its threat to back the US campaign to get international discussion about Iran's nuclear activities out of the UN's nuclear watchdog agency where it belonged and into the UN Security Council, where the US had a veto and which had the power to impose sanctions.

(It should be noted that European business interests have been far less enthusiastic about anti-Iran sanctions than their respective governments. In early 2007, the Anglo-Dutch Shell Oil company signed an agreement with Iran to develop a major natural gas field, in direct opposition to the Bush administration's efforts to broaden the US's economic sanctions to its trade partners, particularly in Europe.[107])

Public opposition to a US strike on Iran is fairly wide, but thin and uneven. While polls show that huge majorities oppose a US military strike on Iran (see next question, "Is diplomacy possible between the US and Iran?") the fear that has blanketed US public consciousness since the horrific events of September 11 has only partially lifted. That fear would likely be intensified—and indeed manipulated—by even a thinly disguised "Tonkin Gulf–style" incident or provocation.

Is diplomacy possible between the US and Iran?

Like virtually every government in the world, Iran's leaders condemned the September 11 terrorist attacks on the US. In his first interview with a US newspaper after the attacks, Iran's then President Khatami called al-Qaeda's version of Islam extremist, and said "the horrific terrorist attacks of Sept. 11, 2001, in the United States were perpetrated by [a] cult of fanatics who... could only communicate with perceived opponents through carnage and devastation."[108] Two days later he called the attacks "the ugliest form of terrorism ever seen."[109]

Despite the ongoing US sanctions still in place against Iran, Khatami's government offered to assist the US and other Western countries in stabilizing Afghanistan. The offer reflected longstanding Iranian opposition to the Taliban, but also a remarkable openness to cooperation with the US. Some in Washington seemed to find it difficult to take Iran's offer seriously, but on the ground it worked. According to James Dobbins, Bush's first post–September 11 envoy to Afghanistan, "perhaps the most constructive period of U.S.–Iranian diplomacy since the fall of the shah of Iran took place in the months after the 2001 terrorist attacks."

In fact, Dobbins' description of the US–Iranian anti-Taliban collaboration provides a fascinating view of what a US–Iran relationship could look like. In a 2007 *Washington Post* op-ed widely seen as part of the efforts by some in the Washington elite to prevent a US military strike on Iran, Dobbins wrote:

> Many believe that in the wake of Sept. 11, the United States formed an international coalition and toppled the Taliban. It would be more accurate to say that the United States joined a coalition that had been battling the Taliban for nearly a decade. This coalition—made up of Iran, India, Russia and the Northern Alliance, and aided by massive American airpower—drove the Taliban from power.
>
> The coalition then worked closely with the United States to secure agreement among all elements of the Afghan opposition on the formation of a broadly based successor to the Taliban regime.
>
> As the American representative at the U.N. conference in Bonn, Germany, where this agreement was reached, I worked closely with the Iranian delegation and others. Iranian representatives were particularly helpful.

It was, for instance, the Iranian delegate who first insisted that the agreement include a commitment to hold democratic elections in Afghanistan. This same Iranian persuaded the Northern Alliance to make the essential concession that allowed the meeting to conclude successfully.[110]

Even for those who do not believe that the US attack on Afghanistan was legal, let alone just, it is revealing to see how those in power inside the administration at the time who *did* endorse that illegal war[111] viewed Iran's role as helpful to Washington's strategic goals.

Beginning before the attacks of September 11, 2001, the US and Iran had been involved in secret high-level talks based on an Iranian offer of unconditional negotiations. Just a few weeks after the 2003 US invasion of Iraq, Iran offered the US a set of new proposals for a comprehensive Middle East solution. Hilary Mann, then a top State Department official, received the message from the Iranians via the Swiss ambassador, who acted as go-between for the US in dealing with Iran.

> Mann was startled by one dramatic concession [by Iran] after another—"decisive action" against all terrorists in Iran, an end of support for Hamas and the Islamic Jihad, a promise to cease its nuclear program, and also an agreement to recognize Israel.
>
> This was huge. Mann sat down and drafted a quick memo to her boss, Richard Haass. It was

important to send a swift and positive response.

Then she heard that the White House had already made up its mind—it was going to ignore the offer. Its only response was to lodge a formal complaint with the Swiss government about their ambassador's meddling.[112]

According to the then senior director of the National Security Council for the Middle East, Flynt Leverett, what Iran wanted in return from the US, beyond some specifics regarding lifting economic sanctions and ending Washington's ban on Iran's entry to the World Trade Organization, was a security guarantee. It was an offer of normalized relations between the US and Iran, something that had not existed since 1979 when the US-backed shah was overthrown. In return Iran wanted a guarantee that the US would not attack, or invade, or attempt "regime change" in Iran. A grand bargain indeed.

The "realists" of the Bush administration, including then Secretary of State Colin Powell were reportedly interested in such a bargain. But they were not able to win against the neoconservative forces grouped around Vice President Cheney and the civilian leadership of the Pentagon under Secretary of Defense Donald Rumsfeld. Assessing responsibility for the lost opportunity, Powell's former assistant, Colonel Lawrence Wilkerson, said, "as with many of these issues of national security decision-making, there are no fingerprints. But I would guess Dick Cheney with the blessing of George W. Bush."[113]

The propaganda efforts of the Bush administration ultimately didn't work. In June 2008, just as John McCain was ramping up his attack on the newly anointed Democratic candidate Barack Obama for "naiveté" in proposing unconditional talks with Iran, a Gallup poll revealed that nearly six in ten Americans believed it would be a "good idea" for the US president to meet with the president of Iran. Two-thirds believed the president should be more broadly open to talking with "enemies" of the US. Nearly half of McCain's supporters (in an anticipated Obama–McCain race) favored direct president-to-president talks with Iran, and an overwhelming 78 percent of Obama supporters said the same thing.[114]

Nor have the consistent US threats prevented Iran from attempting new diplomatic initiatives. In May 2008 the Iranian foreign minister issued a call for wide-ranging international talks without pre-conditions that would include political, security, and economic issues, including Iran's nuclear program and the Arab–Israeli peace process. He did not offer to end Iran's own nuclear enrichment ahead of talks (the deal-breaking demand of the Bush administration), but he did call for establishing "fuel production consortiums" in several countries, including Iran. That proposal, already under consideration in a number of capitals as a way of providing more countries with nuclear fuel without each having to create its own production capabilities, would involve building internationally controlled uranium enrichment facilities in several places, including Iran—and thus would mean a greater presence and more involvement by international inspectors in those locations. The foreign minister's proposal, attached to a letter to the UN secretary-general, also called for broad negotiations to help achieve a "sustainable, democratic and fair" solution for the Palestinians and international collaboration against terrorism, drugs, and illegal immigration. The White House may or may not have been studying the proposal, but Defense Secretary Gates questioned dealing with the Iranian government at all, allegedly because of the "resurgence of the original hard-line views of the Islamic revolutionaries."[115] For the US, apparently, talks could still only take place *after* regime change.

What role does Congress have in approving or preventing any military action against Iran?

After the 2003 US invasion of Iraq and as the Bush administration's threats against Iran escalated, Congress began to take a more active role in the debate, considering and passing a number of measures designed to demonize and escalate pressure on Iran and potentially set the stage for approval of a US military strike. In fact no additional congressional action was needed to maintain economic pressure on Iran, since the sanctions imposed more than a decade earlier were still in place. In May 1995 President Clinton had issued Executive Order 12959, banning US trade and investment in Iran, with the explicit goal of hindering Iran's effort to modernize its oil sector. Little more than a year later, Congress passed the Iran Sanctions Act. (Originally named the Iran–Libya Sanctions Act, the title was amended after the US renewed diplomatic ties with Libya.[116])

But by 2003 anti-Iranian fever had spread far beyond the White House, thanks to pressure from Bush and his allies. Resolutions were introduced in the House and Senate to provide $50 million to Iranian opposition groups including those dedicated to "regime change." The House version also called for escalating sanctions and a "total embargo" supposedly designed "to encourage the people of Iran to bring about a more peaceful and democratic government." A further congressional escalation came in May 2004, when the House passed a resolution calling for the US to use "all appropriate means to deter, dissuade, and prevent Iran from acquiring nuclear weapons" and demanded that other governments impose similarly harsh sanctions against Iran.[117]

In March 2007 the House began consideration of the Iran Counter-Proliferation Act of 2007, introduced by the late Congressman Tom Lantos, long a harsh critic of Iran and an enthusiastic supporter of the Iraq war. It called for new energy sanctions to prevent Iran from obtaining gasoline from abroad—Iran does not have the capacity to refine gasoline itself. The Iranian government had long provided gasoline to its population at heavily subsidized prices, and although the US claimed that the energy sanctions' purpose was to divert money from Iran's nuclear program, the sanctions would certainly have a dramatic impact on the Iranian population. The bill also officially identified Iran's Revolutionary Guard units of the military as a "terrorist organization" and prohibited all commercial dealings with them. The bill passed the House on September 25, 2007, the same day Iranian president Ahmadinejad addressed the UN General Assembly in New York, and the day after his controversial speech to students at Columbia University. The bill included language stating that it did not authorize US military force against Iran. It had still not passed the Senate by the summer of 2008. But the bill was widely interpreted as a congressional attempt to help the Bush administration win public support for military strikes against Iran.

Also in 2007, the House passed the Iran Sanctions Enabling Act of 2007, which authorized state and local governments to divest from any companies that had more than $20 million invested in Iran's energy sector, companies that sell arms to Iran, and from banks or other financial institutions that provide more than $20 million credit to the government of Iran. This bill had been introduced by Massachusetts Representative Barney Frank, one of the most consistently liberal voices in Congress, and was co-sponsored by several other liberal and even progressive members, including Representative Barbara Lee of California, co-chair of the Congressional Progressive Caucus and long an icon of the antiwar movement for her consistent opposition to the Iraq war, as well as her heroic stance as the only member of Congress to vote against the original bill authorizing Bush to go to war after September 11. The liberal view seemed to be based on the idea that economic sanctions, no matter their impact on the Iranian people, would somehow serve as a substitute for war, and that by supporting sanctions they could prevent war. But this analysis ignored the reality of sanctions. Legally, sanctions can be considered an act of war. At the human level, as was so obvious to everyone except the US government in the case of the crippling sanctions imposed on Iraq during the 1990s, economic sanctions affect the civilian population while consolidating the power of elites. Politically, sanctions rarely have the desired effect of turning the population against their own government in favor of the outside powers imposing sanctions, but rather, almost always the opposite. (For more on the effect of Iran sanctions, see "Do US sanctions against Iran work? What are the costs?")

Certainly states and cities had the right to divest from whatever companies they chose without the specific authorization of Congress. But the passage of the bill in the House, despite the lack of Senate passage or presidential signature, did in fact encourage more municipal and state governments to take up local sanctions campaigns—in many cases led by liberal and progressive voices eager to find an alternative to war with Iran. In other cases, and sometimes simultaneously, as was the case in Washington, DC in early 2008, anti-Iran sanctions initiatives were brought to local governments by Jewish community relations councils. In many cases those sanctions efforts were not only opposed directly, but were answered with much broader campaigns to pass local or state-wide resolutions or referenda opposing any US military attack on Iran.

The Senate joined the fray with the Kyl–Lieberman bill, which passed on September 26, 2007. Introduced by right-wing Arizona Republican Jon Kyl and super-hawkish, formerly Democratic, later independent Connecticut Senator Joe Lieberman, it was a non-binding amendment to the defense appropriations bill. The bill matched the House version in naming the Revolutionary Guard a "terrorist organization." But it went much further. The bill stated that it was the "sense of the Senate" that

> it should be the policy of the United States that it should combat, contain and rollback the violent activities and destabilizing influence inside Iraq of the Islamic Republic of Iran, its foreign facilitators such as Lebanese Hezbollah and its indigenous Iraqi proxies; to support the prudent and calibrated use of all instruments of United States national power in Iraq, including diplomatic, economic, intelligence and military instruments in support of the policy… with respect to the government of the Islamic Republic of Iran and its proxies.[118]

Although the bill was advisory and nonbinding, its language was deliberately harsh and clearly designed to increase public fear of Iran.

The Kyl–Lieberman bill also became a focus in the Democratic primary fight then raging. Senator Hillary Clinton, at the time the frontrunner for the nomination as Democratic presidential candidate, had voted to support Kyl–Lieberman, claiming it didn't authorize war but would enhance the US negotiating position with Iran—the same claim she made about voting for Bush's 2002 authorization to use force in Iraq. Over the next couple of months her competitors, particularly liberal Senators John Edwards and Barack Obama, attacked Clinton for her vote, claiming the bill in fact did escalate the threat of war. Obama faced criticism of his own role, however, as he had not expressed unequivocal opposition to the bill until after its passage—and he had not returned to the Senate from the campaign trail to vote against it.

Most of the congressional bills have been more about political positioning and political posturing than they have had actual impact on the US–Iran crisis. But Congress does bear the ultimate power—the power to approve or deny the use of funds to pay for any escalation against Iran. One model for how that power could be used is from the period of the illegal US war against Nicaragua in the 1980s. In 1982, angered by the White House's secret escalation of the unpopular war in Central America, the House passed the Boland Amendment, a rider to the Defense Appropriations Act of 1983. It was designed to cut off funds the CIA and other intelligence agencies were using to carry out sabotage attacks in Nicaragua and to support the anti-government Contra guerrillas. The amendment was neither unequivocal nor absolute. It only prohibited the US government from providing military support that was officially "for the purpose of overthrowing the Government of Nicaragua." But it became the symbol of public anger and the public's demand to end US support for the Contras and their brutal war. The amendment thus imposed an even more powerful check on the White House's war-making capacity—the power of political pressure—than the resolution's actual language required.

Some in Congress have recognized the need for a stronger focus on diplomacy and stronger opposition to military threats. In early June 2008, Congressional Progressive Caucus Co-Chair Representative Lynn Woolsey stated that

> no unjust war ever produced a lasting peace. It hasn't in Iraq and it won't in Iran. Instead of another misguided rush to war we need a diplomatic surge for peace and reconciliation. That is why I have introduced H.R. 5056, the "Iran Diplomatic Accountability Act of 2008," which provides for the appointment of a high-level envoy empowered to conduct direct, unconditional, bilateral negotiations with Iran for the purpose of easing tensions and normalizing relations with Iran. It's far past time to talk. It's essential that we ensure that the same President

who manipulated his way into Iraq isn't allowed to double down and get us involved in another bloody quagmire in Iran. The key to ending the stalemate with Iran is robust and vigorous diplomacy, not another military engagement that will further threaten our national security, and destabilize the region.[119]

The Progressive Caucus simultaneously endorsed the "time to talk to Iran" called by the Campaign for a New American Policy on Iran, combining a June 10, 2008 national call-in day to Congress urging diplomacy with Iran with an opportunity for members of Congress, celebrities, and others to talk directly to average Iranians in Tehran, using a row of '60's-era red "hotline" telephones.

If, despite the NIE's determination that Iran is *not* building a nuclear weapon, and despite Iran's NPT-guaranteed right to enrich uranium for peaceful nuclear power uses, anyone in Congress or the White House remains seriously concerned about Iran's nuclear enrichment capacity and intends to try to negotiate an end to that enrichment, they must recognize that there can be no hope for negotiations limited by preconditions. Serious talks to negotiate a serious agreement with Iran are certainly possible. Iran is likely to consider suspending uranium enrichment in the context of broad talks including such key issues as a US security guarantee against potential invasion or "regime change." But demanding that talks ostensibly aimed at achieving an enrichment suspension cannot begin until *after* Iran has suspended enrichment means the US is not looking for talks, but for a confrontation. An offer to negotiate only *after* the other side has given up the key concession is not a serious offer.

What should—and what could—US relations with Iran look like?

Any serious effort to minimize tensions and normalize relations between the United States and Iran must recognize that negotiations and diplomacy, not sanctions, military threats, or military attacks, must be the basis of the US posture toward Iran. The United States should also recognize that the United Nations, through the International Atomic Energy Agency (not the Security Council), should be the central actor in orchestrating international negotiations with Iran. The United States should agree to be bound by international legal prohibitions as well as the global consensus against any military strike against Iran.

A serious effort to ease nuclear disputes should begin with the US recognizing and implementing its own obligations under the Non-Proliferation Treaty, particularly its obligations under Article VI to move with all other nuclear weapons states toward nuclear disarmament and full and complete general disarmament. As long as the US remains in violation of its own NPT obligations, it will continue to fail in convincing other countries to take their obligations seriously.

Any negotiations between the United States and Iran must recognize what Iran actually wants: a security guarantee (guaranteeing no invasion, no attack on nuclear facilities, and no efforts at "regime change"), recognition of Iran's role as an indigenous regional power, and reaffirmation of Iran's rights under the Non-Proliferation Treaty. Once those rights are internationally affirmed, it will be up to Iran itself to determine whether and with whom they will negotiate on how those rights are to be implemented.

The consequences of the United States having severed all diplomatic ties with Iran since 1979 should be recognized and Washington should move urgently to reestablish full diplomatic relations with Tehran.

The US should stop using the Israeli–Palestinian "peace process" as an instrument to gain regional support for its position in the US–Iran crisis, as it did at the Annapolis conference in December 2007, when a high-profile but do-nothing gathering was used as an opportunity to mobilize more support for Bush's anti-Iran escalations. Instead, it should replace its current uncritical political, military, economic, and diplomatic support for Israeli occupation and discriminatory policies with a policy aimed at establishing a just and comprehensive peace in Israel and Palestine based on human rights, international law, equality, and UN resolutions.

What can we, the people, do to prevent a US war on Iran?

We must increase the political cost for any politician or policy-maker even considering or threatening the use of a military strike against Iran. Centers of power beyond Congress and the White House must be organized to broaden significantly the range of visible and mobilized political opposition, to raise that political price. Key actors in the Iraq antiwar movement—those working to pass Cities for Peace city council resolutions, mayors and governors concerned about the costs of war, state legislators insisting their National Guard contingents be available to respond to natural disasters, military families and veterans, active-duty military personnel, 9/11 families—all must be mobilized into even broader antiwar activism.

Active mobilization against an attack on Iran is crucial. Certainly such mobilization will be challenging, but we must confront and overcome the skepticism about the value of antiwar protest that has been created by years of Washington's rejection of the demands of the even larger and longer-standing movement opposing the Iraq war. We have a huge head start already. By early 2007 the most important and influential antiwar coalitions, including the powerful national United for Peace and Justice coalition, with its 1450-plus member organizations, the internet-focused MoveOn.org, the large membership organizations of Win Without War, and the diverse and disparate locally based Cities for Peace movement were all including "No War on Iran" as part of their demands. That makes the next phase of mobilization—integrating the effort to stop war in Iran into the very center of the peace movement—almost easy. United for Peace and Justice and other groups are already building inter-coalition collaborations against war in Iran, and the work of a diverse array of organizations involved in education, advocacy, people-to-people dialog, confrontation with those in power, local city and state campaigns, and much more, is already cohering into a powerful movement.

The peace movement should also join and support the large and influential Iranian communities across the US, Europe, and elsewhere who are already mobilized against a potential US attack, to develop joint campaigns aimed at preventing a military assault on Iran.

We need more conferences, speaking tours, mainstream media campaigns, teach-ins, alternative media features, educational material, and other resources, all aimed at providing the basic information that will empower these growing movements and political mobilizations against a new war in Iran, and will help ensure their success.

We must fight for more congressional hearings, both official and unofficial public briefings, as well as informal and off-the-record meetings with members of Congress. We should press members of Congress to examine the entire range of Iran-related issues, including the human, military, and strategic consequences of US military strikes there, the consequences in global opinion of the US, the range of possible/likely Iranian retaliation, the inherent violations of international law and the possibility of prosecution of those participating in funding or approving such strikes, and the danger of Tonkin Gulf-style "provocations." The peace movement should continue campaigns for Congress to pass a "Boland Amendment" on Iran aimed at preemptively prohibiting all spending for military force against Iran.

We should encourage wide participation in people-to-people delegations to Iran, and call for congressional and staff delegations to travel to Iran as well, possibly in the context of building parliament-to-Congress relationships.

Certainly, we also need early coordination to mobilize US and global protests following any specific threat of US attack or major escalation of rhetoric, as well as to plan for "The Day After" demonstrations if any attack should take place.

The threat of a US attack on Iran remains real, but it is far from inevitable. Unlike the run-up to the 2003 invasion of Iraq, when the most powerful forces in the US government had already determined to go to war despite widespread public, military, and political opposition, the debate over war in Iran remains wide open. The strong majority agreement across the United States, and the near unanimity in the rest of the world, that the Iraq war has been a disaster for Iraq, for the US, for the region, and for the world, means that there is even less support for launching another, equally or even more disastrous war in Iran. There is still time. We have a powerful movement experienced in mobilizing and we have years of success in changing public opinion. We can do it again. We must.

Notes

1 Peter Baker and Robin Wright, "U.S. Renews Efforts to Keep Coalition Against Tehran," *Washington Post* 5 December 2007.

2 Michael Hirsh, "Bothersome Intel On Iran," *Newsweek* 12 January 2008 <www.newsweek.com/id/91673>.

3 Andrew Gray, "Iranians Threatened U.S. Ships in Hormuz: Pentagon," Reuters, 7 January 2008.

4 "US Warns 'Reckless' Iran," news24.com, 9 January 2008 <www.news24.com/News24/World/News/0,,2-10-1462_2248336,00.html >.

5 Helene Cooper, "Iran Is Fighting Proxy Battle in Iraq, U.S. Diplomat Says," *New York Times* 12 April 2008.

6 Karen DeYoung, "Iran Top Threat to Iraq, U.S. Says," *Washington Post* 12 April 2008.

7 Editorial, "Countering Iran," *Washington Post* 13 April 2008.

8 Zev Chafetz, "Israel Can Stand Up for Itself," *New York Times* 13 April 2008.

9 Nathan Guttman, "Iran Can Also Be Wiped off the Map," *Jerusalem Post* 8 May 2006 <www.jpost.com/servlet/Satellite?pagename=JPost/JPArticle/ShowFull&cid=1145961301962>.

10 Ethan Bronner, "Just How Far Did They Go, Those Words Against Israel?" *New York Times* 11 June 2006.

11 <www.whitehouse.gov/news/releases/2006/04/print/20060428-2.html>.

12 NPT Article IV: "1. Nothing in this Treaty shall be interpreted as affecting the inalienable right of all the Parties to the Treaty to develop research, production and use of nuclear energy for peaceful purposes without discrimination and in conformity with articles I and II of this Treaty. 2. All the Parties to the Treaty undertake to facilitate, and have the right to participate in, the fullest possible exchange of equipment, materials and scientific and technological information for the peaceful uses of nuclear energy. Parties to the Treaty in a position to do so shall also cooperate in contributing alone or together with other States or international organizations to the further development of the applications of nuclear energy for peaceful purposes, especially in

the territories of non-nuclear-weapon States Party to the Treaty, with due consideration for the needs of the developing areas of the world."

13 Atul Aneja, "IAEA Says No Evidence of Iranian N-Weapons Plan," *Hindu* 1 March 2006.

14 Mohammad Sahimi, "Iran's Nuclear Program. Part I: Its History," *Payvand's Iran News* 2 October 2003.

15 "Timeline: U.S.–Iran Ties," BBC, 28 May 2007 <news.bbc.co.uk/1/hi/world/middle_east/3362443.stm>.

16 Peter Baker, "Bush Urges Schroeder to Push Iran on Weapons," *Washington Post* 28 June 2005 <www.washingtonpost.com/wp-dyn/content/article 2005/06/27/AR2005062700334.html>.

17 "Timeline," BBC.

18 Ibid.

19 Michael A. Fletcher and Keith B. Richburg, "Bush Tries to Allay EU Worries Over Iran," *Washington Post* 23 February 2005.

20 Dafna Linzer, "Iran Is Judged 10 Years From Nuclear Bomb," *Washington Post* 2 August 2005.

21 Office of Coordinator for Counterterrorism, US State Department, *Country Reports on Terrorism 2007*, Chapter 3: State Sponsors of Terrorism, 30 April 2008 <www.state.gov/s/ct/rls/crt/2007/103711.htm>.

22 CNN, "Report: Global Terrorism up More than 25 Percent," quoting Russell Travers, deputy director of the National Counterterrorism Center, 30 April 2007 <www.cnn.com/2007/US/04/30/terror.report/index.html>.

23 PBS *Frontline*, "Chronology: U.S.–Iran Relations 1906–2002" <www.pbs.org/wgbh/pages/frontline/shows/tehran/etc/cron.html>.

24 Ambassador Michael Sheehan, coordinator for counter-terrorism, "Post-Millennium Terrorism Review," speech at Brookings Institution, 10 February 2000 <www.globalsecurity.org/intell/library/news/2000/02/000210_sheehan_brookings.htm>.

25 Gareth Porter, "Bush's Iran/Argentina Terror Frame-Up," *Nation* 18 January 2008 <www.thenation.com/doc/20080204/porter>.

26 Nicole Gauette, "Israel: Iran Is Now Danger No. 1," *Christian Science Monitor* 28 November 2003.

27 Uzi Mahnaimi and Sarah Baxter, "Israel Readies Forces for Strike on Nuclear Iran," *Sunday Times* (London) 11 December 2005.

28 Anne Penketh, "Israel Raises Nuclear Stakes with Iran," *Independent* 25 January 2007.

29 "Target Iran: Air Strikes," GlobalSecurity.com <www.globalsecurity.org/military/world/israel/iran.htm>.

30 Ibid.

31 Aluf Benn, "Study: U.S., Israel Should Begin Planning Strike on Iran's Nuclear Sites," *Ha'aretz* 3 December 2007.

32 *Business Finance News* 6 June 2008 <www.iii.co.uk/news/?type=afxnews&articleid=6749120&subject=economic&action=article>.

33 Jad Mouawad, "Oil Prices Skyrocket, Taking Biggest Jump Ever," *New York Times* 7 June 2008 <www.nytimes.com/2008/06/07/business/07oil.html?_r=1&oref=slogin>.

34 Ben Quinn, "Olmert Admits Israel Has Nuclear Weapons," *Telegraph* 13 December 2006 <www.telegraph.co.uk/news/migrationtemp/1536692/Olmert-admits-Israel-has-nuclear-weapons.html>.

35 IAEA Board of Governors, "Implementation of the NPT Safeguards Agreement in the Islamic Republic of Iran," 4 February 2006 <www.iaea.org/Publications/Documents/Board/2006/gov2006-14.pdf>.

36 Elaine Sciolino, "U.S. Compromises on Wording of Iran Nuclear Resolution," *New York Times* 4 February 2006.

37 Author interview with anonymous State Department official at Council on Foreign Relations meeting, March 1999.

38 Luke Harding and Duncan Campbell, "Calls for Olmert to Resign After Nuclear Gaffe," *Guardian* 13 December 2006.

39 "Legality of the Threat or Use of Nuclear Weapons," Advisory Opinion, International Court of Justice, 8 July 1996 <disarm.igc.org/oldwebpages/icjtext.html>.

40 "Pentagon Considering Use of Nuclear Weapons: LA Times," *People's Daily Online* 11 March 2002 <english.people.com.cn/200203/11/print20020311_91867.html>.

41 National Security Council, *The National Security Strategy of*

the United States of America [2002], 17 September 2002
<www.whitehouse.gov/nsc/nssall.html>.

42 Walter Pincus, "U.S. Nuclear Arms Stance Modified by
Policy Study," *Washington Post* 23 March 2002.

43 F. Stephen Larrabee, "Defusing the Iranian Crisis," *Orange
County Register* 9 March 2006.

44 Ewen MacAskill, "Thousands Would Die in US Strikes on
Iran, Says Study," *Guardian* 13 February 2006.

45 Reuters, "Iran: U.S. and Britain to Be Sued," *New York Times*
13 May 2008.

46 "Zbigniew Brzezinski Summary: Iran," Bookrags.com
<www.bookrags.com/wiki/Zbigniew_Brzezinski#Iran>.

47 State of the Union, 23 January 1980, President Jimmy
Carter <www.jimmycarterlibrary.org/documents/speeches/
su80jec.phtml>.

48 "Appendix B—The Glaspie–Hussein Transcript" in Phyllis
Bennis and Michel Moushabeck, eds., *Beyond the Storm: A Gulf Crisis
Reader* (Northampton: Olive Branch Press, 1991).

49 National Security Directive 54, 15 January 1991
<www.washingtonpost.com/wp-srv/inatl/longterm/fogofwar/
docdirective.htm>.

50 Colum Lynch, "Firm's Iraq Deals Greater than Cheney
Has Said," *Washington Post* 23 June 2001.

51 Ali Akbar Dareini, "Iran Ends Voluntary Cooperation with
IAEA," Associated Press, 5 February 2006.

52 Office of the Press Secretary, "President Bush Addresses
the 89th Annual National Convention of the American Legion,"
press release, 28 August 2007 <www.whitehouse.gov/news/
releases/2007/08/20070828-2.html>.

53 "Top Bush Officials Push Case against Saddam," CNN, 8
September 2002 <archives.cnn.com/2002/ALLPOLITICS/09/
08/iraq.debate/>.

54 Ed Pilkington, "Bush Threatens to Confront Iran Over
Alleged Support for Iraqi Insurgents," *Guardian* 29 August 2007.

55 "Iranian Laws, Government, and Policy: The Constitution
of Islamic Republic of Iran: Chapter VII" Iran Chamber Society,
updated 1 July 2008 <www.iranchamber.com/government/
laws/constitution_ch08.php>.

56 Dafna Linzer, "Troops Authorized to Kill Iranian Operatives in Iraq," *Washington Post* 26 February 2007.

57 Karen DeYoung, "Pace Demurs on Accusation of Iran," *Washington Post* 13 February 2007.

58 "Standoff in the Persian Gulf," CBS/AP, 23 March 2007 <www.cbsnews.com/stories/2007/03/23/world/main2600191.shtml>.

59 Julian Borger and Ian Black, "US Strikes on Iran Predicted as Tension Rises over Arms Smuggling and Nuclear Fears," *Guardian* 15 September 2007.

60 "France Warning of War with Iran," BBC, 17 September 2007 <news.bbc.co.uk/2/hi/middle_east/6997935.stm>

61 Scott Peterson, "US and Iran Spar Ahead of Iraq Report," *Christian Science Monitor* 31 August 2007.

62 Dana Perino, Press Gaggle, 8 January 2008 <www.whitehouse.gov/news/releases/2008/01/200801081.html>.

63 William Clark, "Petrodollar Warfare: Dollars, Euros and the Upcoming Iranian Oil Bourse," Media Monitors Network, 2 August 2005 <www.energybulletin.net/7707.html>.

64 "Iran Stops Accepting U.S. Dollars for Oil," RIA Novosti, 8 December 2007.

65 National Security Council, 2006 National Security Strategy <www.whitehouse.gov/nsc/nss/ 2006/sectionV.html>.

66 Antonia Juhasz, *The Tyranny of Oil: The World's Most Powerful Industry and What We Must Do to Stop It* (New York: HarperCollins, forthcoming 2008).

67 Anthony Sampson, *The Seven Sisters* (London: Hodder, 1975). Cited in Juhasz.

68 Juhasz, *The Tyranny of Oil*.

69 Jim Vallette, "Cheney's Oil Change at the World Bank," Energy Bulletin, 30 March 2005 <www.energybulletin.net/5009.html>.

70 Warren P. Strobel, John Walcott, and Nancy A. Youssef, "Cheney Urging Strikes on Iran," McClatchy Newspapers, 9 August 2007.

71 Ibid.

72 "U.S. Plans Base on Iraq–Iran Border," BBC, 10 September 2007

<news.bbc.co.uk/2/hi/middle_east/6987306.stm>.

73 Abdullah Al Shayji, "Iraq's Most Influential Neighbor," *Gulf News* 11 March 2008.

74 Scott Bittle and Jonathan Rochkind, "Energy, Economy New Focal Points for Anxiety Over U.S. Foreign Policy," Public Agenda: Confidence in U.S. Foreign Policy Index, Spring 2008 <www.publicagenda.org/foreignpolicy/ pdfs/foreign_policy_index_spring08.pdf>.

75 Shirin Ebadi and Hadi Ghaemi, "The Human Rights Case against Attacking Iran," *New York Times* 8 February 2005.

76 Human Rights Watch, "Iran: Cooperate With UN Bodies," 6 June 2008 <hrw.org/english/docs/2008/06/06/iran19036.htm>.

77 Golnaz Esfandiari, "Iran: El-Baradei Says Attack On Country Would Be Catastrophic," Radio Free Europe/Radio Liberty, 26 January 2007 <www.globalsecurity.org/wmd/library/news/iran/2007/iran-070126-rferl02.htm>.

78 "Timeline: U.S.–Iran Ties," BBC, 13 January 2008 <news.bbc.co.uk/2/hi/middle_east/3362443.stm>

79 "Hans Blix Questions U.S. Fears over Iran," CTV Canada, 24 October 2007 <www.ctv.ca/servlet/ArticleNews/story/CTVNews/20071024/blix_nuclear_071024/20071024>.

80 AP, "Shut Jail, Ex-Diplomats Say," *Los Angeles Times* 28 March 2008.

81 Fadi Eyadat and Mazal Mualem, "Carter Calls on U.S. to Start Direct Dialog with Iran," *Haaretz* 16 April 2008 <www.haaretz.com/hasen/spages/974880.html>.

82 "Analysts Claim U.S. Military Options in Iran are Not Good," *Daily Times* (Pakistan) 24 January 2005 <www.dailytimes.com.pk/default.asp?page=story_24-1-2005_pg4_21>.

83 AP, 17 September 2007.

84 General Wesley Clark, "StopIranWar.com," Huffington Post, 21 February 2007 <www.huffingtonpost.com/gen-wesley-clark/stopiranwarcom_b_41752.html>.

85 Jonathan Karl and Luis Martinez, "U.S. Commander: Iran Would be 'Disastrous'," ABC News, 28 May 2008 <www.abcnews.go.com/Politics/International/story?id=4949459&page=1>.

86 "Fallon Breaks His Silence," *International Herald Tribune* 4 June 2008 <www.military.com/news/article/fallon-breaks-silence-on-his-dissent.html? ESRC=eb.nl>.

87 Demetri Sevastopulo, "U.S. Admiral Keen for Contact with Iran Navy," *Financial Times* 4 June 2008 <www.ft.com/cms/s/0/d0a02eac-31d0-11dd-b77c-0000779fd2ac.html>.

88 Esfandiari, "El-Baradei Says."

89 Don Phillips, "Iran Sanctions' Risk to Air Safety is Cited in Report," *International Herald Tribune* 13 December 2005.

90 Borzou Daragahi and Ramin Mostaghim, "Iran Sanctions Ripple Past Those in Power," *Los Angeles Times* 20 January 2008 <www.latimes.com/news/nationworld/world/mideastemail/la-fg-sanctions20jan20,0,5447841.story?coll=la-news-mideastemail>.

91 Reese Ehrlich, "U.S. Tells Iran: Become a Nuclear Power," Foreign Policy In Focus, 28 November 2007.

92 Corey Flintoff, "Timeline: Words Fly Over Iran's Nuclear Program," NPR, 4 December 2007 <www.npr.org/templates/story/story.php?storyId=16933380>.

93 General Accounting Office, "Iran Sanctions: Impact in Furthering U.S. Objectives Is Unclear and Should Be Reviewed," December 2007 <www.gao.gov/new.items/d0858.pdf>.

94 Ambassador Doumisani Kumalo, Statement in Explanation of Vote by Ambassador DS Kumalo of South Africa at the United Nations Security Council Vote on Non-Proliferation (Iran Resolution), 3 March 2008 <www.southafrica-newyork.net/pmun/view_speech.php?speech=2483657>.

95 Andrew Cockburn, "In Iraq Anyone Can Make a Bomb," *Los Angeles Times* 16 February 2007.

96 James Glanz and Richard J. Opal, "U.S. Displays Bomb Parts Said to Be Made in Iran," *New York Times* 27 February 2007.

97 Michael Hirsh, "Bothersome Intel on Iran," *Newsweek* 21 January 2008.

98 Terry Atlas, "Six Signs the U.S. May be Headed for War in Iran," *U.S. News and World Report* 23 March 2008 <www.usnews.com/blogs/news-desk/2008/3/11/6-signs-the-us-may-be-headed-for-war-in-iran.html>.

99 Seymour M. Hersh, "A Strike in the Dark: Why Did Israel Bomb in Syria?" *New Yorker* 11 February 2008.

100 "Interview of the Vice President by Martha Raddatz, ABC News," Office of the Vice President, White House transcript, 24 March 2008 <www.whitehouse.gov/news/releases/2008/03/20080324-8.html>.

101 Michael Abramowitz, "Administration Puts Its Best Spin on Iran Report," *Washington Post* 24 March 2008.

102 AP, "U.S. Says 1 Dead in Suez Canal Shooting," 26 March 2008 <abcnews.go.com/International/ wireStory?id=4525857>.

103 Thomas P. M. Barnett, "The Man Between War and Peace," *Esquire* April 2008 <www.esquire.com/features/fox-fallon>.

104 Donna Miles, "Gates Accepts Resignation of CENTCOM Chief Fallon," AFPS, 11 March 2008 <www.globalsecurity.org/military/library/news/2008/03/mil-080311-afps06.htm>.

105 "Fallon Breaks His Silence," *International Herald Tribune* 4 June 2008 <www.military.com/news/article/fallon-breaks-silence-on-hisdissent.html?ESRC=eb.nl>.

106 Henry Kissinger, "The Disaster of Hasty Withdrawal," *Washington Post* 16 September 2007.

107 Terry Macalister, "Shell Defies U.S. Pressure and Signs £5bn Iranian Gas Deal," *Guardian* 29 January 2007.

108 Elaine Sciolino, "Iran Chief Rejects Bin Laden's Message," *New York Times* 10 November 2001.

109 CNN, "Iranian President Condemns September 11 Attacks," 12 November 2001 <www.archives.cnn.com/2001/WORLD/meast/11/12/khatami.interview.cnna/index.html>.

110 James Dobbins, "How to Talk to Iran," *Washington Post* (online) 22 July 2007 <www.rand.org/commentary/2007/07/22/WP.html>.

111 The terrorist attacks of September 11, 2001, were massive crimes—crimes against humanity. But they were not acts of war. The United Nations Charter, the ultimate repository of international law *and* binding in US domestic law since it was ratified by the Senate in 1945, allows a nation to go to war only in two instances: if approved by the Security Council, or in immediate self-defense. Neither of those requirements was met. In the Charter's Article 51, self-defense applies *if* an armed attack occurs, but only *until* the Security Council can meet to determine how to respond. The council met on September 12, and passed

unanimously and with great fervor and solidarity the exact resolution the US had proposed—but that resolution said nothing about going to war against Afghanistan. Not because the US feared that the UN wouldn't approve it, but because the Bush administration didn't want to acknowledge the UN's legitimate right to regulate the use of international force. The council decision called for financial cooperation to track terror organizations—not war or military force. If the Pentagon had scrambled fighter jets to take down the second plane before it hit the second New York tower, that would have been legitimate self-defense. The US invasion of Afghanistan weeks after the attack was not self-defense, and it was illegal. And bringing NATO into the picture, with European and Canadian NATO troops taking much of the burden off US troops so more of them can be sent to Iraq, has not made the war on and occupation of Afghanistan legal. NATO does not have the right to authorize war; only the UN Security Council does.

Afghanistan did not go to war against the United States. A small group of Saudi and Egyptian terrorists did. They didn't live in Afghanistan, they lived in Hamburg; they didn't train in Afghanistan, they trained in Florida; they didn't go to flight school in Afghanistan, they went to flight school in the Midwest. They may have been inspired by someone living in Afghanistan, but that did not give the US the right to invade Afghanistan weeks after the attack. That is not self-defense, and each death of an Afghan civilian caught under US bombs is an additional violation of the laws of war.

112 John H. Richardson, "The Secret History of the Impending War With Iran That the White House Doesn't Want You to Know," *Esquire* 18 October 2007.

113 Gareth Porter, "Neo-Con Cabal Blocked 2003 Nuclear Talks," *IPS/Asia Times* 30 March 2006.

114 Michael D. Shear, Robin Wright and Jon Cohen, "McCain Urges Sanctions, Divestment to Press Iran," *Washington Post* 3 June 2008.

115 Robin Wright, "Tehran Urges New Round of Talks," *Washington Post* 21 May 2008.

116 Ken Katzman, "The Iran Sanctions Act," Congressional Research Service, 12 October 2007 <www.fas.org/sgp/crs/

row/RS20871.pdf>.

117 "Target Iran: Countdown Timeline," Global Security <www.globalsecurity.org/military/ops/iran-strikes.htm>.

118 *National Defense Authorization Act for Fiscal Year 2008*, 110th Cong., 1st sess., H.R. 1585. Available at <www.weeklystandard.com/weblogs/TWSFP/Iran%20amendm ent.pdf >.

119 Press release, Campaign for a New American Policy on Iran, 6 June 2008 <www.newiranpolicy.org/536/29301.html>.

Resources

Books

Abrahamian, Ervand. *Iran: Between Two Revolutions*. Princeton: Princeton University Press, 1982.

Ahmad, Eqbal. *The Selected Writings of Eqbal Ahmad*. New York: Columbia University Press, 2006.

Aslan, Reza. *No God But God: The Origins, Evolution, and Future of Islam*. New York: Random House, 2006.

Benjamin, Medea and Jodie Evans. *Stop the Next War Now: Effective Responses to Violence and Terrorism*. Maui, San Francisco: Inner Ocean Publishing, 2005.

Bennis, Phyllis. *Challenging Empire: How People, Governments and the UN Defy US Power*. Northampton: Olive Branch Press, 2005.

Bennis, Phyllis, and Michel Moushabeck, eds. *Beyond the Storm: A Gulf Crisis Reader*. Northampton: Olive Branch Press, 1991.

Byrne, Malcolm, and Peter Kornbluh. *The Iran-Contra Scandal: The Declassified History*. New York: The New Press, 1993.

Cleveland, William L. *A History of the Modern Middle East*. Boulder: Westview Press, 2004.

Ebadi, Shirin. *Iran Awakening: A Memoir of Revolution and Hope*. New York: Random House, 2006.

Ehrlich, Reese. *The Iran Agenda: The Real Story of U.S. Policy and the Middle East Crisis*. Sausalito: Polipoint Press, 2007.

Falk, Richard. *Unlocking the Middle East: The Writings of Richard Falk*. Ed. Jean Allain. Northampton: Olive Branch Press, 2002.

Gasiorowski, Mark J., and Malcolm Byrne. *Mohammed Mosaddeq and the 1953 Coup in Iran*. Syracuse: Syracuse University Press, 2004.

Gonzalez, Nathan. *Engaging Iran: The Rise of a Middle East Powerhouse and America's Strategic Choice*. Westport:

Praeger SI/Greenwood Press, 2007.

Hiro, Dilip. *The Iranian Labyrinth: Journeys Through Theocratic Iran and its Future*. New York: Nation Books, 2005.

Juhasz, Antonia. *The Bush Agenda: Invading the World One Economy at a Time*. New York: HarperCollins, 2006.

Juhasz, Antonia. *The Tyranny of Oil: The World's Most Powerful Industry—And What We Must Do to Stop It*. New York: HarperCollins, 2008 (forthcoming).

Keddie, Nikki R. *Modern Iran: Roots and Results of Revolution*. New Haven: Yale University Press, 2003.

Kinzer, Stephen. *All the Shah's Men: An American Coup and the Roots of Middle East Terror*. Hoboken: John Wiley & Sons Inc., 2004.

Nasr, Vali. *The Shia Revival: How Conflicts within Islam Will Shape the Future*. New York: W.W. Norton, 2006.

Parsi, Trita. *Treacherous Alliance: The Secret Dealings of Iran, Israel and the United States*. New Haven: Yale University Press, 2007.

Takeyh, Ray. *Hidden Iran: Paradox and Power in the Islamic Republic*. New York: Times Books, 2006.

Articles / Reports / Documents

Clark, William. "Petrodollar Warfare: Dollars, Euros and the Upcoming Iranian Oil Bourse," *Media Monitors Network* 2 August 2005 <www.energybulletin.net/7707.html>.

Ebadi, Shirin and Hadi Ghaemi. "The Human Rights Case against Attacking Iran," *New York Times* 8 February 2005.

Ehrlich, Reese. "U.S. Tells Iran: Become a Nuclear Power," *Foreign Policy in Focus*, 28 November 2007.

Guttman, Nathan. "Iran Can also Be Wiped off the Map," *Jerusalem Post* 8 May 2006 <www.jpost.com/servlet/Satellite?pagename=JPost/JPArticle/ShowFull&cid=1145961301962>.

Hersh, Seymour M. "The Coming Wars." *New Yorker* 24 January

2005 <www.newyorker.com/archive/2005/01/24/050124fa_fact>.

————. "The Iran Plans." *New Yorker* 17 April 2006 <www.newyorker.com/archive/2006/04/17/060417fa_fact>.

————. "The Next Act." *New Yorker* 27 November 2006 <www.newyorker.com/archive/2006/11/27/061127fa_fact>.

————. "Shifting Targets: The Administration's Plan for Iran." *New Yorker* 8 October 2007 <www.newyorker.com/reporting/2007/10/08/071008fa_fact_hersh>.

Klare, Michael T. "The Iran War Buildup." *Nation* 21 July 2005 <www.thenation.com/doc/20050801/klare>.

Leverett, Flynt L. "Iran: The Gulf Between Us." *New York Times* 24 January 2006.

Lowe, Robert and Claire Spencer. "Iran, Its Neighbours and the Regional Crises." Chatham House Middle East Programme Report, UK, 2006 <www.chathamhouse.org.uk/research/middle_east/papers/view/-/id/409/>.

MacAskill, Ewen. "Thousands Would Die in US Strikes on Iran, Says Study," *Guardian* 13 February 2006.

National Intelligence Estimate. "Iran: Nuclear Intentions and Capabilities." November 2007 <www.dni.gov/press_releases/20071203_release.pdf>.

Ong, Carah. "Congress and Iran: 2007 Review and 2008 Outlook." Center for Arms Control and Non-proliferation, 4 January 2008 <www.armscontrolcenter.org/policy/iran/articles/iran_2007_review_2008_outlook>.

Richardson, John H. "The Secret History of the Impending War with Iran that the White House Doesn't Want You to Know." *Esquire* 18 October 2007 <www.esquire.com/features/iranbriefing1107>.

Sturm, Frankie. "The Candidates on Iran," *Foreign Policy in Focus* 4 April 2008 <www.fpif.org/fpiftxt/5122>.

Office of Coordinator for Counterterrorism, US Department
of State. *Country Reports on Terrorism 2007*
<www.state.gov/s/ct/rls/crt/2007/>.

White House. "The National Security Strategy." March 2006
<www.whitehouse.gov/nsc/nss/2006/>.

Websites

"A Country Study: Iran." Library of Congress
<www.memory.loc.gov/frd/cs/irtoc.html>.

PBS *Frontline*, "Chronology: U.S.–Iran Relations 1906–2002."
<www.pbs.org/wgbh/pages/frontline/shows/tehran/etc/cron.html>.

"Target Iran: Countdown Timeline," GlobalSecurity.org.
<www.globalsecurity.org/military/ops/iran timeline.htm>.

"Timeline: U.S.-Iran Ties," BBC, 28 May 2007
<www.news.bbc.co.uk/1/hi/world/middle_east/3362 443.stm>.

The National Security Archive. "The Iran Documentation Project"
<www.gwu.edu/percent7Ensarchiv/iran/index.htm>.

Organizations

US

After Downing Street (www.afterdowningstreet.org)
American Friends Service Committee (www.afsc.org)
Campaign for a New American Policy in Iran (www.cnapi.org)
Center for Arms Control and Non-Proliferation
(www.armscontrolcenter.org)
Cities for Peace (www.citiesforpeace.org)
Code Pink (www.codepink4peace.org)
Faithful Security (www.faithfulsecurity.org)
Fellowship of Reconciliation (www.forusa.org)
Global Policy Forum (www.globalpolicy.org)
Hague Appeal for Peace (www.haguepeace.org)
Institute for Policy Studies (www.ips-dc.org)

Just Foreign Policy (www.justforeignpolicy.org/iran)
National Iranian-American Council (www.niacouncil.org)
Nuclear Age Peace Foundation (www.wagingpeace.org)
Peace Action (www.peace-action.org)
StopWarOnIran.org
United for Peace and Justice (www.unitedforpeace.org)
>   (United for Peace and Justice is the largest antiwar coalition in the US. Most of the organizations listed above are constituent members of UFPJ.)

CANADA
Canadians Against War (www.canadiansagainstwar.org)
Canadian Peace Alliance (www.acp-cpa.ca/en/index.html)
Canadian Voice of Women for Peace (www.home.ca.inter.net/
~vow/)
The Council of Canadians (www.canadians.org)

AUSTRIA
International Atomic Energy Agency (www.iaea.org)

UK
Network for Peace (www.networkforpeace.org.uk)
Stop the War Coalition (www.stopwar.org.uk)

THE NETHERLANDS
Transnational Institute (www.tni.org)

SWEDEN
The Weapons of Mass Destruction Commission
(www.wmdcommission.org)

INDIA
Coalition for Nuclear Disarmament and Peace
(www.cndpindia.org)